Make a Joyful Noise

Also by Dr. Bobby Jones with Lesley Sussman

Touched by God:
Black Gospel Greats Share Their Stories of Finding God

St. Martin's Press ❧ New York

Make a Joyful Noise

My 25 Years in Gospel Music

Dr. Bobby Jones *with*
Lesley Sussman

MAKE A JOYFUL NOISE : MY 25 YEARS IN GOSPEL MUSIC.
Copyright © 2000 by Dr. Bobby Jones with Lesley Sussman. All
rights reserved. Printed in the United States of America. No part
of this book may be used or reproduced in any manner whatsoever
without written permission except in the case of brief quotations
embodied in critical articles or reviews. For information, address
St. Martin's Press, 175 Fifth Avenue, New York, N.Y. 10010.

www.stmartins.com

Book design by Victoria Kuskowski

Library of Congress Cataloging-in-Publication Data

Jones, Bobby.
    Make a joyful noise: my 25 years in gospel music / Bobby Jones
with Lesley Sussman.
        p. cm.
    ISBN 0-312-25258-7
        1. Jones, Bobby. 2. Gospel musicians—United States—
Biography.
    3. Television producers and directors—United States—Biography.
    I. Sussman, Les, 1944–   II. Title.

ML420.J753 A3 2000
782.25'4'092—dc21
[B]
                                                              00-040254

First Edition: November 2000

10   9   8   7   6   5   4   3   2   1

To my beloved friend Ethel; my brother, James; my sister, Lula;

and my dear friend Vickie. They are the four pillars of my life,

whom I lean on and depend upon

for strength in good times and bad.

Contents

Acknowledgments · xiii
Preface · xv
Introduction: A Little House on a Hill · 1

1
Grandma, and a Three-Room House with No Toilet · *5*

2
Alcohol Breaks Up a Family · *13*

3
"Elephant Ears" Bobby Jones · *21*

4
A Three-Fingered Piano Player · *31*

5
Hard Lessons in St. Louis · *39*

6
Back to Nashville · *51*

7
Oprah and Project Help · *55*

8
The First Black Expo, the Reverend Jesse Jackson, and
Some Other Friends · *59*

 Contents

9
A Star Is Born · *65*

10
Barbara Mandrell Defies the Rules · *75*

11
Guided by Spirit · *79*

12
Betrayed · *89*

13
Fear and Loathing in South Africa · *101*

14
Gospel-Music Legends and Good Friends · *109*

15
Some Sour Grapes Over
My Grammy Award · *123*

16
Forgiving My Father · *131*

17
Two Costume Changes in a Funeral Casket · *141*

18
Marriage Was Not in the Stars · *153*

19
Minister Farrakhan Buys Me a Bottle of Cologne · *157*

20
An Explosion of Gospel Music · *165*

21
I Baptize Al Gore's Wife · *171*

22
My Soul Mate, at Last! · *175*

23
Bonding with Kirk Franklin, and Awed by Aretha · *181*

24
Pastor T. D. Jakes Offers Me Comfort · *191*

25
Bringing My Mother to Jesus · *197*

Epilogue · *201*

Acknowledgments

There are so many people who filled crucial roles in my life and career that it would take an entire book to list them all. Some very special people I'd like to single out are:

Maya Angelou, Barbara Mandrell, Aretha Franklin, Minister Louis Farrakhan, the Reverend Jesse Jackson, the Reverend Al Sharpton, Bob Johnson, Eva Childress, Lydia Jones, Johnnie Thorpe, and Dr. Ruby Martin at Tennessee State University. All these generous people helped to lift my sights and were always there for me.

As far as my career is concerned, I'd like to acknowledge television station WSM-TV in Nashville. Without them I would never have been able to do what I am doing today.

I'd especially like to thank Theresa Hannah and Nettie Stowers, who suggested that we produce a gospel show on that station. I want to thank Theresa despite the fact that our relationship was seriously damaged at one time.

I must also offer my gratitude to the McGraw-Hill publishing company for what it did to promote a shy black man's confidence to speak before large groups of people. They were the launching pad for my career.

One very special person to whom I will always be grateful is Bob Johnson, president of Black Entertainment Television. From the very beginning, he believed and supported my efforts in bringing gospel music to television.

I also want to extend my thanks to Gerry Jones, who worked so hard with me to help me build my career, and to Azell Futrell, who is one of my closest and dearest friends and has worked with me for twenty-five years. And a special thank-you to Derrick Lee, my current music director.

I also want to mention the First Street Baptist Church in Nashville, where I met Mrs. Eva Childress, who became like a godmother to me when I first arrived in that city.

Let me also thank my agent, Claire Gerus, for making this book possible, and Glenda Howard, my gospel music–loving editor at St. Martin's Press.

Last, but not least, much thanks to Les Sussman, the writer to whom I told my story. I can't say enough about Les, who spent many patient hours helping me to set the record straight. But for the life of me, I still can't figure out why God sent a white guy to help me write my memoirs.

Preface

The *real* Bobby Jones, offstage, is pretty much what people see on television when they tune in to my show each week. I'm as much that friendly, warm, and congenial person in my private life as I am in my professional one. That sometimes surprises people when they meet me in a personal setting, although I don't know what else they'd expect from a charming guy like myself!

But there are other aspects to my personality as well. And that's one reason why I wrote this book. I want people to really get to know the heart of that person who comes into their household on a regular basis. After more than twenty-five years in the gospel music business, I felt it was time for my fans to learn things about me, like where I came from, the challenges I've faced in my life, where I now live, and even what I think about while I'm shaving in the morning.

Do I do drugs? (No!) Am I a woman chaser? Am I married? Am I insecure? Has doing my show always been easy street? You will find answers to these and many more questions about my personal and professional life as you continue to read this book.

This book is also written to help inspire young people who may be experiencing some adverse situation in their lives. I want them to know that I also experienced adversity when I was their age, and still managed to have a rich life, a quality life.

My struggles centered around my alcoholic father who was sometimes abusive and often failed to give me the love I so desired. Nowadays, however, I prefer not to use the word *struggles*. Instead, I like to call them *challenges*; words like *struggles* and *problems* connote something else altogether to me. *Challenge* is a more accurate word—it indicates that the situation is conquerable. I overcame those challenges and I know that any youngster reading this book can do the same if he or she so chooses.

Another important reason for writing this book is that I wanted to tell my story of all the hard work that went into becoming the successful celebrity that I am today. Some people who watch my show think it all came to me easily.

But nothing was handed to me on a bed of roses. I worked hard to get to where I am, and I made a few enemies along the way. But I was fortunate to be touched by God, who has always guided me in all my undertakings. Everything I've accomplished—my doctorate degree, my career in gospel music, the satisfaction of having the longest-running gospel-music show in the history of television and being the first person to ever have a gospel show named after him—all are the result of a combination of hard work and God's grace.

Like my last book, *Touched by God*, which is the story of the spiritual struggles of many of gospel music's top stars, this book is also important to me because it helps to promote the gospel-music industry which I love and feel strongly connected to.

I'm glad to have another opportunity to talk about the history of gospel music, and to introduce you to two women who are among its pioneers: Willie May Ford Smith and Sallie Martin. They go all the way back to the days of Dr. Thomas A. Dorsey, a visionary who put a new face on gospel music in the 1930s.

For those readers who are more interested in the modern crop of gospel-music stars, you'll find plenty to read about in this book. Over the years I've met and become friends with many of today's current stars—everyone from Kirk Franklin, whom I introduced to the gospel-music world on my show—to the Williams Brothers and Aretha Franklin.

I'll tell you everything I know about these artists, including some surprising stories, like the day I playfully chased Shirley Caesar down a hotel hallway and the time that Al Green showed up to tape my show, acting a bit strangely.

There are other familiar faces who also appear in this book. They may have no direct connection with gospel music, but they're dear friends of mine and powerful leaders of the African-American community. They include the Reverend Jesse Jackson, Oprah Winfrey, Maya Angelou, the Reverend Al Sharpton, and Minister Louis Farrakhan.

In addition, you will meet celebrities who are white folks but also longtime friends—people like Barbara Mandrell, who did as much for me as anybody in show business, country-music star Ronnie Milsap, and even Tipper Gore, who I baptized in the Jordan River.

Over the years, I've done a lot of traveling around the world to promote gospel music. I've even been dubbed by some people as "the Ambassador of Gospel Music."

In this book I will share with you some stories about the incredible journeys I've been on—from the Holy Land where Jesus once walked, to the dangerous terrain of South Africa at the height of apartheid, where my life was often in danger.

Not only have I faced dangers during some of my travels abroad, but here in my own country as well. Few people know, for example, that shortly after the assassination of Dr. Martin Luther King Jr. I was arrested in Nashville for no other reason than being a black man who happened to be driving through the streets. I was unceremoniously thrown in jail and spent several frightening hours in the downtown police lockup.

There is much more you will learn about me and the personalities who make up the world of gospel music in the pages of this book. But the final thought I'd like to leave you with is that Bobby Jones is a guy who is at peace with himself.

I'm someone who is in love with the Lord, his chosen mate, his work, his ministry, gospel music, and, especially, his millions of fans around the world. I don't know what the next twenty-five years will bring, but for as long as I can, I hope I'm around to help use my television ministry to reach out to those fans in order to build our Kingdom of God.

—Dr. Bobby Jones
Nashville, Tennessee
January 2000

Make a
Joyful Noise

Introduction

A Little House on a Hill

The asphalt highway unwinds like a black snake into the darkness before me as I speed toward the Henry County General Hospital in Paris, Tennessee, where my mother has just died.

It's Saturday night, and seated next to me is my sister Lula, her eyes moist with tears. I glance at the clock on the dashboard of my car, and it says it's almost seven o'clock. But as far as I'm concerned, time has stopped and no longer holds any significance for me.

It seems only moments ago that my sister and I were dining in a small nearby restaurant. There wasn't much to talk about—it's hard to keep up a lively conversation when one's mother lies dying in a hospital bed. Besides, my sister was never much of a talker. I think I was telling Lula about my upcoming concert tour—I was on my way to Italy—when the waiter came over to our table and told me I had a phone call.

My heart sank and I feared the worst. I knew that at this hour it was not a business call. Looking at the expression on my sister's face, I could see that she was sharing the same anxious thoughts.

I had been expecting bad news, but until you get it you just don't know what your feelings are going to be. On the phone, the attendant at the county hospital gently told me that my eighty-year-old mother had just passed away.

What could I say? I remember hanging up, feeling on the one hand a certain sense of relief—my mother would no longer suffer now that she was in Jesus' hands. I also recall thinking that a lot of people lose their parents at a much earlier age, and we were blessed to have had our mother alive for a long time.

But what I remember feeling most of all was gut-wrenching grief.

It was 6:38 P.M. on April 4, 1998. That year I was fifty-nine years old.

I was Dr. Bobby Jones, a respected educator, Grammy Award winner, successful recording artist, and host of a gospel music television program seen weekly by millions of people from coast to coast and around the world.

I was also that shy kid who had grown up dirt-poor in a three-room house on a hill just outside of Paris, Tennessee, with no electricity or running water, and sometimes not enough food to eat. But despite all my professional success, right now I was feeling miserably alone.

My mother's death came at a time of my life when more doors were opening for me than ever before. I was at a point where everything was going the way I would have it go. Now a door had slammed in my face. One that would never open again for me.

Life now made me look at it in a way I had never been forced to do before. Because now my mother was dead, and I would never recover from that fact. From this time on I would have to face life without my dearest friend and adviser.

Most of my life had been spent trying to please my mother and to make her proud of me. So when she passed away my energy was sapped to a degree that I would never recover from—even though I'm a Christian and realize that we should celebrate death instead of mourning, because we go to Him.

Even, today, I still mourn her loss. She gave me, my brother, and my sister so much love and support in our later years. Now that I've lost her, I feel as if I've lost part of me as well.

Still, something positive has come out of that experience. I have learned to deeply cherish and appreciate those special people who are still in my life. Nowadays, whenever I feel sad, I concentrate on these people and I feel gratitude to the Lord for having blessed me with them.

Watching the dark ribbon of a highway unwind before me as I drive toward the hospital, I'm haunted by memories—some of them not so sweet. There are painful memories of a childhood spoiled by an abusive, alcoholic father, and of a mother who during my early years also succumbed to alcohol and sometimes found it difficult to return the deep love her young son felt for her.

There are good memories, too—of a brother and sister whom today I love dearly; memories of how I eventually found the love I so desperately sought from my mother, and how close we became over the years. Happy memories, also, of my eventual reconciliation with my father in the final years of his life, and the closeness and love we began to feel toward each other. There are other sweet memories that flit ghostlike through my mind—of the wonderful places around the world that I've been, people I've known and cared for, and of all the divine guidance I've received that has contributed to who I am today.

Watching the highway unfurl before me, I can't help but wonder where this road will lead me tomorrow. But mostly my thoughts drift back to a little dot on the state map labeled Henry, Tennessee, and a little house on a hill where it all began, some sixty years ago. . . .

Grandma, and a Three-Room House with No Toilet

I was born about two-thirty A.M. on the eighteenth of September, 1938, in my grandmother's house in Henry, which is in the western part of Tennessee, all the way up near Kentucky. Henry had a population at that time of about five or six hundred black people. I was the last of three kids, and my grandmother and a couple of her cousins were there to deliver me.

My grandmother was a midwife and she delivered all of us. I remember that she was a medium-sized woman, very brown skinned and very stately. Her name was Lydia Jones we called her Mammy Lydia—and she was very respected in the community.

Mammy Lydia told me that as a baby I was absolutely gorgeous, and that everybody loved me. She said I was fair-skinned and had nice curly hair. Those were the typical characteristics blacks wanted to have at that time because it was perceived that you would be treated better. It was terrible having to grow up living like you were nothing because of the color of your skin, but that's the way it was—and in some places of the world today, still is.

My mother, Augusta, was in her twenties when she had me. She had been fourteen years old when she had my older brother James. I think my father, Jim, was sixteen or seventeen when he married my mother. He had met her in town during some social situation.

Both of my parents' families were sharecroppers. Sharecropping was all you could do if you lived in the country. That's what my grandparents did, that's what my parents did, and that's what I did as a kid.

Jim Jones was a nice-looking man with fair skin and sandy hair. My mother was tall, brown-skinned, and gorgeous. I remember that she always kept everybody laughing and she herself had this wonderful laugh. People loved her. They would come around just to hear her laugh.

My mother and my father didn't have much money. Both my mother's parents died when she was very young, so she was raised by her stepmother and her brothers. My father's mother was a single parent because her husband left home when my father was very young.

My mother had seven or eight brothers and sisters and my father had five—and most of them on both sides died violently, especially on my father's side. One of his sisters was killed by her husband—shot to death. Another sister went to the funeral and on her way back to St. Louis was killed in a car wreck. A couple of others died under mysterious circumstances.

My parents were just kids when they got married, but that was typical. In those days, most people got married at fourteen or fifteen. Today when kids get married that young we look at it as bad. But it depends on the times you're living in. Back then it was good for my mother to get married at fourteen because she had someone to take care of her.

They were in love. I know that, because even after she left my father as a result of his heavy drinking, she eventually took him back. She lived with him until he died and never again wanted to leave his side.

The house in Henry that I grew up in was wood-framed and it stood on top of a hill. It was my grandmother's house and we all lived there. Even when my family moved out, I stayed there with my grand-mother until she died.

I stayed with her because I wanted to—a lot of it mainly having to do with my father's drinking problem and the stormy relationship that my sister and I had with my parents. I'll tell you about that a little later.

Mammy Lydia's husband had left her, but her father was still alive at the time—he didn't die until he was 102 or 103 years old. He also lived with us in that house. He was blind and his name was Aintney Dinwiddie.

I remember that the house had three rooms and there was a dirt road leading to it. In the winter it was real hard to get in or out. My grandmother's house was the same size as the house my parents later built just down the hill from us on land they inherited. There was no electricity or other conveniences in my grandmother's house, and we had an outdoor toilet.

In my mind's eye I still see my grandmother cooking on a wood-stove. There was no well, so we had to haul the water in from town in a rain barrel. It was very poor living conditions, but we kids didn't know we were poor, we made the best of our circumstances, and we were proud that we did own our land and our houses.

Mammy Lydia was responsible for my developing years. I went everywhere with her, and everything I did was with her. It was always "Bob and Mammy Lydie."

I don't know how the name Bobby got on my birth certificate, because my aunt had named me Bob and that's the name I grew up with. I remember being teased about it. Kids would tell me that I didn't have a real name—that my *real* name was Robert or Bobby. My aunt said, "I named you Bob and it's not Robert or Bobby and all that."

I still remember how I would pick berries and nuts and clean up the graveyards with Mammy Lydie. That's how she made some money, and I would help her. We would get up early in the morning and she had this passionate desire to go to the cemetery. We would always make sure the cemetery was kept clean. I knew everybody's grave. I would get out there and pull the bushes and make sure the grass was cut on the graves. We used a sickle at the time—we didn't have lawnmowers. The berries that we picked, we would sell for a dollar a bucket. My grandmother would sell them to the white people in the area. I would go with her and that's how we made our money for the summer.

These were the first white people I ever saw. We didn't know anything about segregated communities back then. You just lived where you lived. If somebody white lived there, then they usually owned all the land around. Black people would have a house on that land, and to pay for living there, they would work the fields.

I guess I remember being mindful that white people were different than we were, and that we had to be subservient to them. My father would say, "Yes sir" and "No ma'am" even if the white people were younger than he was. I was always curious about that.

One day when we were coming back from the fields I asked my father about that: "That man sure was mean to you and you kept saying, 'No sir' and 'Yes sir' to him and you acted like you were afraid of him. And he was younger than you. Why did you do that?"

"That's the way it is," he replied. "They're the ones that have everything and we have to work for them."

I felt a lot of love in my grandmother's house, and my parents didn't mind that I stayed there. They lived just a few doors away and my uncle Clyde Dinwiddie lived across the hill, so the family was pretty much together.

I'm told that as a kid I was always very inquisitive. I wanted to know where I was born and what time and under what conditions. And while my sister was very quiet and my brother kind of moderate in his behavior, I was outgoing. I think I got that personality from my mother.

I wasn't at all shy at that age. The shyness came later. In fact, I was pretty aggressive. My mother said I was always into things and causing things to happen. I guess I was what you would call a mischievous child.

Another thing I remember is my mother telling me I was a quick learner. She told me early that I was gifted. I was always able to learn things faster than my older brother and my sister.

Church Singing and Jitterbug Dancing

As far back as I can remember, I was singing. I used to have a real high voice. I would stand on tree trunks and my dogs would be my audience. And I would sing away.

I would sing at school and at church. My mother always made us kids go to church. We were Methodists. And my brother and sister, they could sing, too. My mother could sing a little bit, so I think my talent came from her.

There's a few things I remember about my church—although I can't remember its name. It was an old frame church, and I remember when a new building was put up that I was a major part of the choir. My sister and I were somewhere between seven and nine years old, and Sunday after Sunday we were the two featured soloists. I was known as a singer even as a little boy.

It was a real opportunity to sing in the church and lead the choir. It gave me a good platform to practice singing, and I realized that I had a skill that I could use. I also remember how people would come up after the service and compliment us for our singing. Then I started putting together a quartet and we sang church music.

Even though I had singing talent, there wasn't very much encouragement from my parents about furthering my singing ability. At that time education wasn't a real focus. The law stipulated we had to finish school, and most of the kids waited until they were sixteen, quit school, left the area, and headed north. Most of them headed toward Indianapolis. That's where most of my cousins went. Also to Chicago and St. Louis. My brother was a quick learner, so he went on to high school and graduated. My sister didn't go on beyond high school.

It wasn't only singing that I was good at. My sister and I also used to be excellent dancers—but this was outside the church. We used to dance because my mother and father were drinking and going to little joints around Henry. My sister and I would be hauled in there, so we learned how to dance. We listened to the popular music on the jukebox and we would dance for a nickel a dance. We would do the jitterbug and make some money.

Every weekend we'd be in those bars, watching our parents drink. Sometimes we asked to go because we wanted to be with them. And I remember that sometimes it would be eleven or twelve at night and we were still there. It wasn't a good environment for us at all.

Just Churchin'

I grew up in the Methodist church in Henry. They would teach the proper behavior that a Christian should have, and they put the fear of God in me. But it wasn't done in a heavy-handed way, because Methodists are very subdued. I also learned all my Scriptures there.

There was also a sanctified church in Henry that our family sometimes would go to. It was way down by the railroad tracks and it was a form of entertainment for us to get into town where there were some stores—not like where we lived, which was just country—and to see the saints in that church, which we didn't have in our own.

So we would walk about a mile to where the stores were and another mile to get to the church. We'd stay there until nine or ten at night and then walk all the way back home. I remember that we'd walk in clusters, and we'd have fun running, talking, and laughing. The grown folks would walk together, and the kids would be playing up and down the road. Walking back, it was pitch-black and you'd do all the things kids do in the dark. We'd jump out at each other and things like that.

That sanctified church had a lot of music going—tambourines and other instruments. I really wanted to join that church because of the music, but I didn't understand them speaking in tongues or the holy dances they used to do.

I got up one of the nights of their meetings, and I went to the front row. I was thinking about joining that church because a couple of my cousins belonged to it. I wanted to try to speak in tongues like they did, so I fell on the floor and made up some sounds. We were laughing about it all the way home. I don't think I was really all that serious about joining the church.

But I do remember that church and school were the center of my activities. We would go either to the Methodist church or the Presbyterian church. We alternated Sundays because there weren't enough people in the community for them to conduct services each week on their own.

I can still recall how we used to dress up on Easter. We didn't make a big to-do about Christmas as far as church was concerned, although we'd have the Christmas trees and give away presents. But Easter was the big day we all dressed up for. Everybody had to have something new to wear.

Christmas was about toys and people getting drunk at parties. It always seemed strange to me that people would get intoxicated during such a holy time. I remember one Christmas when I was about nine or ten. My mother bought me a little suit and a beret. One of my best friends had the same beret. I was so mad about that, I think I got into a fight with him.

2

Alcohol Breaks Up a Family

My parents' drinking habits made me hate weekends. It was on weekends that tumultuous experiences would happen—especially with my father if he was able to get hold of some alcohol.

My father had a serious alcohol problem that disturbed all of us and broke up our family. He was a quiet man until he became intoxicated. I think he used alcohol to bury his grief.

He was uneducated and couldn't read or write. My mother had to take care of any situation that required reading or writing. And my mother would drink, too. The two of them would just break our hearts that they were unable to control themselves.

And it was embarrassing—publicly embarrassing. My father was so rude to us once he started drinking, and sometimes my mother would be in the same state of intoxication. It seemed to me that everybody in town drank. Some of them could handle it and some of them couldn't. There were quite a few men who were my father's drinking buddies, and some had more control than he had. But a lot of them, like my father, would display their ignorance on the weekends after they'd been drinking.

Those weekends were always an ordeal for us. If my father had a rifle or a gun around the house, he would chase us with that, and he would threaten to fight my mother all the time. It was just chaos during the weekend. During the week everything was fine. But come Friday evenings, that's when we knew to get ready for a serious and disturbing weekend. And that happened almost all of my life until I got my mother to leave him. I was eleven years old and in high school when that finally happened. I was one of these bright kids who started high school at eleven and finished when I was fifteen.

I remember that my sister and I—my brother was off to school—tried to protect my parents when they were out drinking. We'd follow them around and try to make sure they didn't get hurt. That's why today it upsets me to look at people who are in an intoxicated state. I pity the person who allows himself or herself to get into that condition.

In some ways I think my parents' alcoholism was a turning point in my life. When my family moved to the town of Paris, Tennessee—I think I was about eleven—I knew that I didn't want to live with them. I started becoming independent and looking out for myself. I already had started making plans to do something else so I wouldn't have to be exposed to that anymore.

Another thing that came out of that situation is that my sister and I vowed that we would never drink like that. And, thank God, we haven't.

It also caused a deep division between my father and me because of the way he treated us and our mother when he was intoxicated. He wasn't a good role model for me, and I used to look to other men—like my cousins and uncle—for someone to look up to. And he knew that.

I think that experience gave me low self-esteem. And it's something I still suffer from. Millions of people who watch me on television don't know that I'm very shy. But I am, because of the words that were said to me by both my parents when I was young. Some of those things were so painful, I've tried to forget them. But when your parents say something ugly to you, it's difficult to ever forget those hurting words.

How can you forget a father who calls you a "son of a bitch," or threatens to "kick your ass"? He'd shout at me—"Get your ass out of here!" And when I refused—especially when I didn't feel like doing field work—he would say things like, "You sissy, you're lazy, and you ain't gonna amount to anything." But I always stood my ground.

I think that's one of the reasons why my father and I didn't get along so well. He wanted me to learn the skills of plowing and doing the things he knew to make a living, and I resented that and didn't do it well. Then he'd look at me disgustedly and say "I hate you." I didn't keep my mouth shut. I'd tell him, "I hate you back." It was terrible. I think he and my mother loved my brother and sister more than me because they were passive and didn't speak back. But I didn't take much from either of them.

Maybe that's one reason why I've been so successful in my professional career. Their treatment of me was so painful that it became a challenge for me to show them I was better than what they might have thought of me. I think I set out to prove a point: that I wasn't the failure they said I was. If I hadn't had that challenge set out in front of me, who knows what I'd be today? The Lord has a way of working everything out.

I've always been very smart. Even at that age I understood the situation, and I always tried to make excuses for it. I was also a very proud person. I always wanted to be in the best situation; I didn't want anybody to have a better mother or a better father than me, or a better living situation than I had.

So I tried to straighten things out. One way I tried to bring a little harmony into my life was by staying with my grandmother for so many years. All our houses were next to each other, so it wasn't that I could really escape from what was happening with my parents, but I tried to. I grew up living in both houses, but I slept in my grandmother's house. It was a more normalized living situation.

When my grandmother died, I was really heartbroken. She had provided a support system that I would miss. I couldn't turn to my sister. She was passive, and when my parents would go on one of their binges, she wouldn't say much, but just look sad. I would voice my anger and she would keep still.

Nor could I turn to my brother for any solace. He had gone off to school. I was eight years old when I was going through all this, and James was sixteen and in college. Even though I wished he was there for me, I still thought that was very sharp. I was impressed that at a time when kids in that area didn't go to college, he had the desire to succeed. I think he probably set the desire in me to want to do the same.

Nowadays, when I think back to that time, I realize that my parents loved me but just weren't able to express it. They would try to show it, yet it wasn't like they would say to us, "We love you," and words like that. Still, I remember feeling kind of rejected—especially by my father.

Despite such tensions between us, as the years passed and my father grew ill, things eventually changed between us for the better. I'll talk about that more, later on in this book—about how we eventually came to know, love, and respect each other. Even at this writing, and long after his death, I still think about him. I continue to miss him deeply.

Cotton Fields and Saturday-Afternoon Baths

I hated chopping and picking cotton and whatever the chores were in the field with a passion. We would leave for the fields about seven in the morning and get back home about five.

But I tried to turn it into a good time. Even though it was hard work and I despised it, us kids would fool around and try to invent fun for ourselves. And lunchtime was great. I enjoyed eating lunch in the fields—especially if there was something good to eat.

I remember that sometimes the people who owned the crops would pick up a number of us and we'd work with different crews in different fields. And we'd find time to joke and talk about all kinds of things. It was fun meeting these people because it gave me somebody new to talk with and be around.

When we were at home, we'd listen to the radio whenever we

could afford batteries. And because we had no running water, we wouldn't take a bath until Saturday. We would wash up in the washpan.

My mother used the water from the rain barrel to cook with, and we had to ration some of that water for bathing. If there was a drought or it didn't rain, we didn't have water, so we'd have to borrow a horse and wagon and take our barrel downtown. We'd pay two dollars for a barrel of water and we had to be careful coming back because of the rough roads. Some of the water would slosh out of the barrel, and sometimes the barrels would turn over if you didn't drive the wagon just right. You had to ease down the hills—and there was an art to that.

A One-Room Country Schoolhouse

Our elementary school in Henry only operated during the winter months, because the spring and fall were harvest times. The school kept to that schedule to accommodate our parents—who were mostly farmers. There was no school after August so that we could gather the crops.

There were about thirty to forty kids in our one-room school-house—all of them black. The grades ran from one through eight. There was one teacher who was also black. It was totally segregated, and that didn't change until the 1960s.

I can still remember the first day I went to school. It was 1943 and the war was just starting. It was lean times for everybody, but we didn't really understand that. Our houses were on the hill just across the high-way from where the school was located. I was about five years old and I showed up that first day wearing short pants. I couldn't wait for school to start because I wanted to learn *everything*. Even as a little country boy the idea of learning and being with adults was intriguing to me. I was always an eager learner.

So there I was with the other kids, and I remember the teacher asking me to read something. I read it and then the teacher asked me to do my numbers. I did those, too. "He's too smart," she said to the other kids. "I'm going to move him to the second grade." I remember being so excited about that. These were older kids, but I still excelled in everything except science and math. They were challenging subjects for me. I loved history and social studies—those were my favorite subjects. And I also loved reading.

Recess also was a favorite time for me. We'd go and play ball. I was a good athlete. We didn't have football at that time, so we played basketball and baseball. We couldn't afford real baseballs, so we made our own out of rags. I don't remember doing much singing in school. It was in church on Sundays that I did most of my singing.

Raising Pigs, and Cold Winters

Thinking back to my boyhood, I guess what I still remember the most about those days is the hill I grew up on and what a lonely place it was. The closest kids were over the hill a good distance away. We didn't even have a telephone. There was one telephone in town, and you had to pay a dime to use it.

I also remember that we didn't own anything but our land. We had no animals to pull a wagon, and we had some food but not the best. We raised a lot of the food that we ate in our gardens—we had two of them, one by my grandmother's house and one by my parents' house. The soil was not very productive, as the land was passed down to us from other people in the community and it was eroded, so we couldn't farm our property.

My family raised pigs and chickens because we needed something to eat. But we didn't have a cow, so we lacked milk. And I would have to get up early in the morning and feed the hogs and chickens and cut the wood for the cooking and heating. I remember that in wintertime it was very cold.

We'd have to huddle up in a room and try to stay as warm as we could because we had one stove to heat the whole house. When we went to sleep, we heated bricks and wrapped them with cloth and put them at the foot of our beds to keep our feet warm. We would use a lot of quilts and blankets to stay warm.

I still have vivid memories of having to walk to town to buy groceries when we needed something that we weren't raising. What a big joy it was when I got my first bicycle! I could get to town faster. And I loved to go in those stores and look at all the things that were sold there. Sometimes when I had a nickel I'd get an orange drink or a Moon Pie.

On the way to the stores or heading back home, we'd go past the houses where the white folks lived. We admired the fact that they didn't have to sit around a stove. They had furnaces. My sister and I used to say that one day we'd have a big house like those white people.

I remember how black men would sit on the side of a building, and how I often hung around, listening to them talk. They'd talk about this and that and the other. Saturdays, we'd go to town, and there was a little park in front of the train station where everybody would be sitting on the cabooses. I loved to be in the midst of the men, listening to them talk about women and life. That was a great time for me.

Those were sweet and bitter times. The sweet times mostly having to do with my grandmother—going to the graveyard, picking berries and nuts, and being under her guidance. The bitter times had to do with my father—his drinking and his abusive behavior.

3

"Elephant Ears" Bobby Jones

The years quickly passed and I soon found myself attending Central High School in Paris, Tennessee. As far as I remember, I liked it there, although there were some tough times and lots of teasing. I went there from the time I was eleven years old until I graduated when I was only fifteen.

Back in Caton Elementary School in Henry, I had already read books written by famous writers like Louisa May Alcott and William Shakespeare. There was a whole series of those books and I would read them over and over again. In high school, I continued to enjoy reading. I also liked geography. But I hated mathematics. I wasn't good in math, but I was good with reading and spelling and I had language skills.

During my school years, all my teachers were good ones. Whether it was my elementary school teachers in Henry, or high school teachers in the town of Paris, they gave us the best they had. But they had good discipline and good parental involvement back then. If you messed up, you would get your butt whipped—both by the teachers and your parents.

I guess I was always one of the bright kids. I was always the leader in whatever happened. I was in the middle of everything. But there was a price to pay for being so smart; it made me appear different and I was teased for it. I was also teased because I was from the country and young and aggressive. I was into everything at the school. They teased me because my clothes were ragged and because I had hand-me-downs and makeshift stuff that was shabby.

The first day I arrived at Paris Central High school is a memory that remains a clear one for me. I can still recall how we pulled up in this bus from Henry, and the students who lived in the city would stand outside the school building and tease all us kids from the country.

The Paris kids would taunt us: "Here come the country folk." The high school had buses coming from all the little surrounding towns—places like Cottage Grove, Mansfield, and my own little town, Henry.

But there were a lot of kids from the surrounding areas that went to country schools like I did, so we were kind of supportive of each other and we managed to get through that kind of stuff.

That first day, I remember getting off the bus and thinking how strange it felt for me to be registering for classes. I also remember being so young, and how eager I was to become part of the mix.

The first thing I got teased about was how I looked. My dad had cut my hair so my head looked pointed—a pointed head toward the center, and big ears. They called me "Elephant ears" Bobby Jones.

Also, I just didn't speak the way everybody else did. I could never really figure out why, because my father was uneducated and my mother had gone to school only through the eighth grade. My brother was smart—the first one to graduate from high school—but he wasn't around, and none of my uncles or cousins had gone to high school. So I didn't have those influences, but I still talked in a more educated way than the other students. I was branded by people in school and in the community for that. They called me "sissy Bob," and it really offended me.

I think one of the reasons why I spoke differently from my peers was that I had this fantasy about being on television. When I was fourteen, I had managed to save enough money to buy my first TV set. And I remember watching that TV set and knowing, that someday, I would be on it. I really wanted to be a newscaster, and so I used to practice that. I think that was part of the reason why I was so ostracized when I was a kid. I was already trying to talk like I was on television.

Another thing I remember is that although I was on the small side, and shy, I was a strong youngster. And I was from the Thorpe and Jones families—the two families from my mother's and father's sides, who had reputations in the community as being mean. They would fight at the drop of a hat. So the students knew about that and they didn't mess with me too much because of the reputation of my families.

We moved to Paris, Tennessee, the second year I was in high school. Before that, I can still remember the long ride from Henry on the schoolbus, and how very tiring it was. It was a dusty ride in the summer and very cold in the winter.

We had to meet the bus at seven o'clock in the morning and we had to walk a mile to where the bus picked us up. Then we rode at least an hour on back roads, picking up other country students. The return trip was also exhausting. By the time my sister and I got home from school, it was usually dark. That was one reason why it was hard for me to get involved in extracurricular activities at the school. There was no way to get home. So if the high school had anything going, like a basketball game—which I did play—I'd have to find a ride.

I loved basketball. I was on the team and I played as a forward. My friend Kenneth Atkins and I were the best on the team. He was also my protector, because, as I said, I was small and shy. If it hadn't been for Kenneth, things probably would have been a lot worse.

A Good Voice, But Bad Clothes

I remember that one day, because I could sing, they put me into the high-school singing group to sing for the "New Farmers of America." We were all black students.

The "Future Farmers of America" was the white youths' farmers' organization, and the girls were called the "Future Homemakers of

America." All the state schools would participate—the event was held once a year in Nashville.

My mother bought me a suit, but she didn't put cuffs on my pants. So there I was onstage, with a big suit and the pants rolled up. I was wearing a shirt that was too big and a tie that didn't look good. The other kids would joke that the way I looked was the reason why we lost the competition. It still hurts to think about how one day my teacher just got up and talked about how bad I had looked. The whole school just ridiculed me, and I went home to tell my mother.

"The teacher talked about me because I didn't dress right," I told her. "The teacher said that's the reason why we lost." My mother looked embarrassed. "You didn't look that bad," she said. I remember that she went off to have some strong words with my teacher.

Messin' Around with Gospel Music

As a kid we didn't have gospel music or really know anything about it. On the radio station at home, mostly what we heard was country music. There were no gospel-music radio stations back then, but once in a while you'd hear a gospel tune. We just sang what we called "black church music." It mostly came out of the hymnals that we had from the Methodist church. My sister and I sang that music all the time, and I led the choir, but we just knew it as black church music.

Probably my first introduction to gospel music came from the music I heard in that Pentecostal church in Henry—they called it "sanctified music." It was a lot different from ours. In our church it was basically the choir that provided the music, but in that sanctified church there was all this rhythm in the music, and much more participation from the audience. It sounded like the whole church was singing together. There was a lot more glee. It was an early form of what we call, today, gospel music.

Even in high school I knew very little about gospel music. I'd heard similar music over the years—like in the sanctified church—but I didn't put a name to it. I didn't know if it was called gospel or what. All I knew was that it had a nice flavor to it and that it was Christian. Because I was so interested in singing, I went ahead when I was a junior in high school and tried to develop several little singing groups who could perform that kind of music. I remember that one of the first groups I formed was called the Gospel Harmonizers, and we messed around with gospel music a little bit. We had nothing but a desire to sing, and this was a good vehicle for us to do it.

The first gospel singer to influence me was Alex Bradford. He was from New Jersey, and for many years he toured Europe as the star of a show called *Black Nativity*. And he had an unusual voice. His range was seemingly limitless. It's amazing, but I can still remember his voice so clearly! I remember hearing him on the radio back in Paris, Tennessee. I even remember the song he sang—"Too Close to Heaven." I just fell in love with it. Then I heard one of my high-school friends, Roland Atkinson, play it on the piano. Roland had studied some music and could play by ear or by sight. And, again, I became attracted to that song.

After high school, when I started attending college in Nashville, that's when my involvement in gospel music grew stronger. But right then, it was just messin' around with the gospel sound a little bit.

Girls, Teachers, and a Love of the Arts

In high school, there were some girlfriends here and there, but nothing really serious. I didn't have any sexual encounters, because I was into finishing college before I got involved in a serious relationship. We'd mostly do things like go to dances. As I said, I'd gotten into dancing from going to the taverns with my parents. But I always had girlfriends. Even when I was a kid there was some fooling around in the barn with Willie Smith, who was my first girlfriend, and then, Lizzy Puckett, and later, Betty Lou Dunlop.

In high school I learned a lot that contributed to who I am today.

Those loving, caring teachers helped to give me some sort of solid foundation and life skills. There was the love of language that I got in English classes, and performance skills that came from always singing with the high-school choir.

The traveling I did with the basketball team helped me to learn how teams work together—something that still serves me well with my business. And I learned about life from the plays I performed in—I was always the leading character in those school plays.

Maybe our high school didn't have the best textbooks or things, but it did give me and the other students enough of an education to compete in the world when we left and moved to other places. And most important, the teachers, the principal, and the parents were all involved and concerned about education.

I'd say that all my artistic interests came from those years and from some of the teachers, but I don't think that back then I was really into the possibility of being an entertainer. I recall that as a youngster living in Henry, I once said that "one of these days" I would be a big star—but I said that to the cats and dogs I was singing to. As I got older, I never thought much about that. I was just trying to figure out something to make a living. I even had this fantasy about becoming a doctor.

My Mother Leaves My Father

I mentioned that my family moved from Henry to Paris in my second year of high school. That happened because things did not get better with my father's drinking.

It was after one of my father's rages—I was about twelve years old— that my sister and I decided we were really tired of all that, and convinced our mother to leave. We had a cousin who lived over in Paris, and she was living with her boyfriend. They had two rooms and they let us come and stay in one of their two rooms for about a week or so—until my mother could find an apartment for us.

I felt relieved that my mother had listened to us and agreed to leave.

I felt that once we were away from that abuse, we were going to have a much better life. I had grown to hate my father for what he had done to us. We called what we were doing an "escape," and we felt good about it.

I remember feeling that now I wouldn't have to go through the burden of listening to him threaten us and having to be around him drunk. Soon after we arrived in Paris my mother found a job working in a white woman's kitchen. She didn't have many skills, so her choices were extremely limited.

We moved into a house in Paris. The woman who rented it to us had six rooms and we had three rooms. We shared the house with her and that's where I lived until I graduated from high school. I think we paid nine dollars a month to live there, and my mother stayed in that house until I graduated from college.

The family my mother worked for was Jewish. They were very warmhearted people, and many times provided food and clothing for us. Initially, I didn't know they were Jewish, I just knew they were white. About the only thing I knew about Jews then was what I used to hear my father say—that there was a place in Chicago that was called "Jew Town." That's about all I knew about Jews; today, I count many of them among my dearest friends.

My father never really bothered us. I think he tried to get my mother to come back once or twice, but nothing came of it. Now I was the father of the family. I was only eleven years old.

My sister and I went to school, and I found a job when I just turned fourteen. I worked as a dishwasher in a restaurant called Paris Landing. The restaurant was located in a state park—it's still there—and it was my first job.

I began working as a dishwasher, then worked up to being a waiter. And when I became a waiter I made quite a bit of money for that time—maybe twenty dollars a week. My sister also found a job, so the three of us had found ways to take care of ourselves.

A Country Boy Graduates

Graduation from high school was a major time for all thirty-two of us who had made it through the four years. It was 1955 and I was seventeen years old. I was one of the leaders of the graduating group, but I wasn't the valedictorian. I was, however, in the top five of my graduating class.

None of us discussed much about what we were going to do after graduation because it was the normal procedure for us to get married or find a job. But I knew one of the guys—he was the valedictorian—who was going to college.

So I put it in my mind that I was going to do the same. I had also decided that it was going to be Tennessee State University in Nashville. When I told my mother, she didn't discourage me. She encouraged me. But she let me know that she couldn't afford to take care of my tuition. "I'm not able to send you to college," she said, "but your uncle might be able to help you pay your first tuition."

I said, "I'll do it on my own." I was always smart enough to figure out a way to make some money. I knew I could find something to get me through. So I stayed with my uncle Johnny Thorpe, which meant I didn't have to pay for room or board. And he loaned me money for my tuition.

I repaid him by taking care of the house and helping him with his construction business. We did brick laying, pouring concrete, repairing floors in homes, building garages and sidewalks. It was hard but honest work.

Some Not-Too-Happy Memories

I don't think I'll ever be able to forget the sadness and embarrassment I lived with from the time I was about eleven to fifteen years old. I

was embarrassed about where we lived, and by what my father was—
an alcoholic. Some of the kids at school knew about that.

I was embarrassed about not having any money to do things. If
there was a play or something at school that my sister and I wanted to
participate in, we would have to stay over with some of our friends
who lived in Paris. That was kind of embarrassing—to not have enough
bus money to get back home.

I had a lot of sadness in that period. I couldn't wait to get out of
Paris and go somewhere like Nashville. I knew that I could hide myself
in Nashville. It was a big city and nobody there would know my business or the humiliation I was going through with my family.

4

A Three-Fingered Piano Player

I was living in my uncle Johnny's house in Nashville and just starting college when I learned how to play the piano. My aunt Willie had a piano, and she loved to play and sing. I did, too. She would have me on the piano stool next to her and we'd just sing. You could hear us all over the neighborhood.

I liked playing the piano, so I'd mess around on the keyboard and see if I could pick out some chords. Eventually I taught myself how to play it with three fingers. And the more I practiced, the better I got. I even learned to play a couple of church songs. Listening to my aunt play—she was very good, and I was trying to get to be able to play like her—I got caught up in her music. It was gospel music.

Then I started to listen to gospel music on the radio. In Nashville they played that kind of music on the radio—not like in Paris, where the stations were filled mostly with country music.

So that's when I first began to identify the gospel-music sound. I remember once going to a Baptist church and they had a gospel choir which was much different than a singing choir. They really rocked my boat.

I think one reason why I was attracted to this style of spiritual music is because I noticed it drew more people to church on Sunday, and that they had more good singers in their choirs. These gospel choirs were also younger and their music had more appeal to young people. And in the back of my mind I was thinking how I would like to attract people to church through whatever musical talents I might have.

I also started seeing groups like the Caravans, and different church choirs. I already had a knowledge of quartet groups because they were on the radio on Sunday mornings in Nashville—groups like the Jewel Gospel Trio, which sang and played keyboards. I remember that trio had a young lady named Candy Staton; she later became a secular artist. At the time she was only singing gospel. And in Nashville I heard one of my first mass choirs. They called themselves the BC&M Choir. They were excellent!

One Sunday there was an announcement on the radio that they needed a piano player for the First Street Baptist Church's Sunday school. I told my aunt I was going to go try out for it.

So I found my way to the church. I played three or four little songs that I'd learned, but I really couldn't really play anything well except "Jesus, Keep Me on the Cross"—and I could only play it with three fingers.

The woman—her name was Mrs. Elizabeth James—hired me. It wasn't exactly for my musical ability but because I was this nice young guy. And that was my first entrée into the gospel-music industry.

In church, I met a woman who sang in the choir, by the name of Eva Childress. It was the beginning of a great relationship. She became a second mother to me—my godmother. Ms. Childress was single and she took me in and gave me my own apartment.

Mrs. James also loved me, so I soon started playing for the senior choir. And from the senior choir I took over the whole musical operation. And I was still just playing by ear.

It was just like a godsend to get me involved in gospel music. It all began to come together for me. Both these women rallied to me and fed me and clothed me all through college. They took good care of me.

And then I started playing for other churches. Our choir sang two

Sundays a month, and the other two Sundays I would play for another church. I was very excited about the music.

It was a lot different from the Methodist church that I came from. I continued to go to gospel concerts and listen to some of the great singers. At that time you didn't have to pay to go, you just gave a donation.

Taking the Teaching Path

My decision to become a teacher was made while standing on the registration line at Tennessee State University. Before that, I didn't even have any real idea what I would major in. I wasn't even sure what a major *was*.

I remember being on that registration line and getting the times and days for my classes when I heard this guy behind me talking about majors. I started talking to him and he explained it all to me. He said:

"What are you majoring in?"

"I don't really know," I told him.

"What are you going to major in?" I asked him.

"Elementary education."

I looked at him and thought about it for a couple of minutes. "Okay, that's what I'm going to major in, too."

So that's when I decided to major in elementary education and become a teacher.

Almost Run Out of Town

In Nashville, while attending the university, I lived with my aunt and uncle for about nine months. Then I moved out because I was able to support myself. I was getting paid to play piano at various churches, working construction with my uncle, and waiting tables in Nashville restaurants.

I had become a good waiter and I was very personable with people. I remember that there was this young white girl who came in every day to eat at this one particular restaurant I was working at in a state park. She and her mother and brother were from another state and they were on vacation.

Well, I became infatuated with this girl. In the basement of the restaurant they had one of these picture machines where you put your quarter in. So we took our picture. After the family returned home, I wanted to send her the picture.

I got her address and didn't realize it was the wrong address. I had included a letter with the picture expressing my love for this beautiful girl and it came back to the hotel. Someone gave the letter to the superintendent of parks—a white guy—and that resulted in one of the most frightening experiences of my young life.

One morning he called me upstairs. He was a big and burly white man. Looking at me with an angry expression on his face, he said:

"Did you write this letter?'

"Yes, sir," I replied.

He continued to glare at me. "Don't you know better than to write a letter to a white girl?"

"She don't live in the South," I told him, frightened but defiant.

He grew angrier. "She's still white. You shouldn't have written that letter. You got five minutes to get off this property or you're either goin' to jail or I'm gonna kill you."

It scared me to death. I thought he would have me killed because that was one of the things that blacks weren't allowed to do in the South—address a white girl in any kind of way.

He was probably just trying to scare me, but it was a very frightening moment in my life. So I rushed home to get my things. I didn't even tell my mother about it. I only told my sister.

I packed some clothes, ran to the main highway, and thumbed a ride. The rest of that summer I stayed with my uncle in Champaign, Illinois. By the time I came back I never heard anything more about it.

Lonely Days, Lonely Nights

Even though I now had a major, I didn't know what I was expected to do at Tennessee State University. College was a complete mystery to me. I remember going to my first classes, but I didn't know much about anything else that went on at a university. I still had that country-boy state of mind.

It took me awhile to get adjusted. My memories of those university years are basically of going to classes and gaining experience about college life. Mostly, I loved the athletic events and the semester breaks when I would return home to visit my mother.

Going to college was a truly wonderful experience for me. These were inspiring and encouraging years with none of the torment that I had experienced in high school. Best of all, I was able to hide myself in the masses of people. Nobody knew about my home life and what I was running from.

Although at church I was the center of attention, in college I could melt into the crowd. I had good advisers and instructors. But that first year still was difficult because, despite all my problems with my family, I missed being away from home.

I was also lonely because my best friends were still in high school. There was my cousin Joan, and Baby Sis, and Peggy, and Kenneth, and Leroy—people I would sing with and run around with. I can still recall being so desperate to get back to them. I also missed my mother. I would go see her at Christmas, Thanksgiving, and Easter. She was living by herself at the time because my sister had gotten married.

I also missed my high-school basketball games and being with my friends and teammates on Saturdays. So I quit the university after only two semesters. I wasn't doing well in class because I was lonely and distracted. I also found some of the subjects too difficult to concentrate on. I dropped out.

At that time my sister was having a baby, and so my excuse for leaving college was that I needed to go home and take care of my sister and her newborn child. I returned to Paris and didn't come back to Tennessee State University until the following fall.

What brought me back was that I knew a couple of my friends would be attending there. Peggy was going on to college, and also my cousin Joan. College now became bearable. I had two good friends to hang around with. I just admired and loved them to death, and we enjoyed each other and the other students.

Peggy and Joan were beautiful girls and the boys on campus were crazy about them. I always wanted them with me because they were so pretty; they made me look good. Paris was known for its beautiful girls—a lot of light-skinned girls and mulattos.

I remember that Peggy got a job in the cafeteria, so she fed me for free. And working at the churches gave me money to pay for my tuition. The teachers continued to be good to me, and my grades came up. I made the honor roll and my grades never dropped off again.

Once I got past those first and second years, then I really got into the groove of knowing what I was going to do. That's when I really knew I wanted to be a teacher.

A Musical Life

I also started bringing all my friends to church. My godmother, Ms. Childress, loved the idea that I was doing that. She loved to cook, and every Sunday I'd bring a group of college kids to church so they could hear me play and hear the choir sing, and afterward she would cook for us.

Between college and my church activities, I got to know a lot of people in Nashville. I was introduced to all the pastors and church choirs. And my choir was one of the tops. I wouldn't have it any other way. I always wanted to be the best in everything!

When I was in my senior year in college, the pastor of the First Street Baptist Church got a little jealous of me. The choir had become so powerful, that I think he felt I was becoming too much for him to handle.

To avoid any continued squabbles, I quit the choir and went to another church—the Cleveland Street Baptist Church. Ms. Childress supported everything I did, and she understood why I quit. And she was the leading woman of the church.

This was a period when I really developed my love of music—especially gospel music. I don't think there was any other musical format that interested me. It was a time when I got to explore and experiment and do so many different things with groups and choirs.

A College Diploma

It was 1959 and I was really excited. There weren't too many people from my little town that went to college—let alone graduated. I was really proud of myself.

I was only nineteen years old, and I now had a bachelor's degree in elementary education. Thinking about my future, the idea of being an entertainer was not part of my plan. I knew that I would be teaching. If I did any playing or singing, it would be in side jobs that had nothing to do with my career. My career was in education.

There was also a girl I was dating—Virginia Mayo—who I thought I would marry. She was very pretty and I spent all my time with her. Virginia and I had known each other in high school, and the last two years that I was at Tennessee State University she was taking classes there.

We dated until I graduated from college, and then I left for St. Louis. Our relationship ended there. I was always amazed that she went for me. I was a plain-looking boy who wore these big glasses and was a studious type.

The other college boys would try to coax her away from me, but that didn't happen. Those years at Tennessee State University were good years for me. It gave me room to be me. It was a great experience.

5

Hard Lessons in St. Louis

Just before I graduated from college, one of my instructors had already lined up a job for me in an elementary school in St. Louis. The school was scouting for teachers at the time, and I was recommended by the head of my department.

During that summer of 1959 I also bought my first car. I remember getting my uncle Johnny to co-sign for me so I could get that car. I told him I'd pay him back because I'd be teaching and would have some money. So he co-signed for me and I bought a blue Chevrolet.

I didn't know how to drive, so I got a friend of mine to drive me to St. Louis. There was a woman in that city who was a preacher—she was an aunt to one of my instructors at Tennessee State University—and I was going to stay with her.

When I arrived, I remember thinking how big and consuming the city was. But I managed to find my way to her house and from there to a school on the north side of the city, called Farraguet Elementary School. It was in a white neighborhood with mostly white students. I arrived at the school and went to my first meeting for the teachers.

I was young and excited that I had a job of my own and that I was going to earn four thousand dollars a year. But I still had a hard time struggling to make ends meet. For one reason or another, something would always happen—like my car needed to be repaired—and I wouldn't have enough money. I can also recall buying my first couch for my apartment, and a secondhand TV. It was only a room, but I was so happy having it.

The kids I was teaching were almost as old as I was; it was the fifth grade. I was about nineteen and they were about twelve. It was a challenging period for me. They were older kids and so I had to learn how to discipline them. The other teachers who had classes were strict disciplinarians, and there was always order in their classrooms. And I wanted to be sure my kids were the same way.

I think the thing that changed the situation and gained me the most respect from those students was when I taught my class how to sing. I was teaching them some songs for Christmas and I taught them three-part harmony. I remember that the principal was walking by the room at that moment and he heard the music and loved it. It was a creative approach and it worked out well.

There was a couple of times when my mother came to St. Louis to visit me and I'd bring my mother to my school. The principal would tell her all about me teaching the kids to sing. I developed a great relationship with him.

St. Louis was also a time in my life when I was kind of wild. I was about nineteen or twenty years old and excited about going to clubs and bars. Part of it was that I was just a kid and going places and doing things for the first time.

It was a time of life when I wasn't focused. I wasn't really doing anything outlandish—I was always kind of disciplined and controlled—but I found myself spending a lot of time in places like bars and bowling alleys. I was also partying hard for many years.

Then something happened. I'm not exactly sure what, but something hit me. I began to look at my life and felt that I should stop going to these places. I felt I had no business being in that kind of environment. Maybe it's because St. Louis is a very ruthless city, and I was afraid of getting into some serious trouble by hanging out in those places.

Crime was something I hadn't experienced in life before, and perhaps I sensed my own vulnerability. Whatever the reason, I said to myself that I was going to change my lifestyle. And I remember starting to make those changes. I was determined to make a drastic change in my life.

I also decided to get another degree. I wanted to be more serious about my course of study. I think I began to grow up. Nobody can tell you when it's going to happen—it just happens.

Thinking back, maybe the decision to change my lifestyle came one day while I was on my way home from St. Louis. I had time driving down there to think about my life and what I wanted to do with it. I recall thinking that I didn't want to end up like my father. I think my maturity developed right then and there. It was do or die. I was going to change my behavior because I saw it wasn't leading me anywhere.

On that drive I also remember thinking a lot about St. Louis and how much I hated that city. It was so big and cold, and meeting friends was difficult there. It had taken awhile before I made any friends there. Then I finally found a church I could play gospel music for in the suburbs. It was a little Baptist church in a town called Braden, with about seventy-five people in the congregation.

I developed great relationships within that congregation, and that became my base for friends in St. Louis. I lived in that city for seven years before I returned to Nashville, and I was teaching all that time.

If anything positive came out of my St. Louis experience, it was that it brought me a certain sense of wisdom. I became streetwise, and that helped me to understand people more.

Before St. Louis I was still really a country boy all the way through. I assumed everyone who said they were a friend of mine had my best interests in mind. But actually that was never the case. I didn't know that, so I had to learn that hard lesson, which I did in St. Louis.

That lesson was brought home to me when some people I had thought were friends broke into my home and stole almost everything.

That happened several times. It was friends who did it, or somebody I had met. Those were challenging experiences, and I learned a lesson the hard way about trusting people.

St. Louis also helped me grow as far as being a teacher is concerned. I learned a lot. It gave me experience about how to deal with negative and positive people. Living and teaching in St. Louis exposed me to all kinds of people. Some were helpful and some of the experiences I had with them weren't so good.

Some Unsettling News Back Home

I'd only go home to Paris, Tennessee, from St. Louis on holidays, because I hated going back to that city. It took me fifteen or twenty years of returning to Paris before I would let anybody know I was there when I returned home to visit my family. I didn't want to meet anyone who lived there.

I hated that town for a lot of reasons—especially because of my parents' drinking habits and all the ridicule that had caused me when I was young. I also had bad memories of being taunted by the other boys because I was an ugly kid with big bumps on my face, and their always teasing me because of the way I talked and the clothes I wore. Those memories didn't go away and they made me hate Paris.

This particular winter, when I got home, my mother told me that she wanted some money to buy her own house. She also told me that she and my father were getting back together again.

I was shocked. I didn't want her to go back to him. But she told me my father had been staying with her and that although he was still drinking, he was no longer abusive.

"I think maybe I should go back to him," she said.

"I don't want you by yourself with him, unless you think he's going to be okay," I told her. "It's up to you."

"I think he's going to be okay," she said. But my mother was wrong.

On that trip home I talked to my father. It was strained, because I didn't like him—I hated him. I said hello to him and tried to avoid him. He knew I didn't like him, and that was upsetting to him.

He tried to make up to me, but I was very obstinate. He wasn't abusive, but he was still drinking. I just didn't trust him after all these years. Then, much later, just before he got sick, he did become verbally abusive again. He would be in the background cursing and being incoherent. Only years later would our love for each other spark, and by then my father was close to death.

A Close Encounter with Death, and a Gospel Group Is Born

There was a time in St. Louis when I was driving up this street and this guy jumped into my car and held a knife to my throat. He said, "Give me all your money."

It scared the life out of me. He said, "You better drive downtown. Take me downtown." And I knew that once we got there, that would be the end of me. So we got halfway downtown and I'm thinking, *This guy can't outsmart me.*

I pulled up to this stop light and spotted a cop. I opened the door, jumped out of the car, and ran through oncoming traffic. I was shouting, "Police, police!" And this guy jumped out of my car and started running the other way.

I got back into my car and drove off to my apartment. I remember sitting in that car and thanking God for saving my life. I think this experience helped to push me into an even more spiritual lifestyle.

Shortly after that I started singing with a gospel group I had put together. We called ourselves the Meister Singers. I got the word Meister, because at Tennessee State University there was an elite singing unit with that name. There were three girls, myself, and a keyboard player. It was a wonderful group.

We worked like professional singers and, for a time, I thought that's what we would become. We were working toward that. We had these pretty robes and we started to be asked to perform at major church programs.

Our professional hopes ended when the lead singer in the group got married and we had to break up. We tried to go on a little without her, but it just wasn't the same. So the group dissolved and I went back to concentrate on my teaching.

Caught Up in Gospel Music

The Meister Singers became good personal friends of mine. Claude, who was a great piano player, and his sister Retha, became another family for me while I was in St. Louis. This went on until 1966, when I returned to Nashville for another teaching job.

Claude would take me to places like the Keil Auditorium to see gospel-music performances. I had gone to see some gospel shows before, when I was going to school in the Nashville area. I had even seen the Caravans perform when Albertina Walker was still with them, but I never went to see gospel-music shows in a consistent manner the way I did when I was in St. Louis with Claude.

We'd go to the Bethlehem Baptist Church on Washington Boulevard, where they had gospel musicals on Sundays, or we'd go to those Keil Auditorium concerts sponsored by radio station KATZ in St. Louis.

I remember once seeing Dorothy Love Coats and the Gospel Harmonettes, and thinking that she was one of the most exciting performers I'd ever seen. I never saw people respond the way they did to her singing. They would shout and jump around and fall down all over the place.

When I saw Dorothy at the Keil Auditorium, she was headlining the show. This was during the 1960s, when three little black girls in a church in Birmingham, Alabama, had been killed by some white people. Dorothy was talking about it and everybody was paying close attention to what she was saying because Dorothy was from Birmingham.

And she had a lot to say that day about the evils of segregation and how the white man was treating blacks during that period.

Then she went on to sing "I'm Just Holding On and I Won't Let Go"—it was one of her favorite tunes—and the people in the audience were just going wild. I thought she was an incredible performer, and I followed her career for many years.

I still remember that her group had these red robes and there were splashes of red everywhere onstage. The same lady who made those robes for her, later on designed the robes for my own gospel group. But that day I remember that you couldn't see anything but red on the stage.

I never did get into any in-depth relationship with Dorothy Love Coats. Years later, when I had my television show, I talked to her a couple of times on the telephone. She called me and told me that she admired my work, and she talked about how poorly she felt the gospel-music industry had treated her. That was in 1976. In talking to her, somewhere along the line I found out that Elvis Presley was using material from some of her songs and not giving her any credit.

She said not only had Elvis taken advantage of her, but other artists and record labels as well. She told me that several record companies whom she had recorded with had used her materials and not given her any royalties for songs that she had written. Dorothy said she was disappointed with the music industry in general.

I remember trying to support her and telling her that I understood her situation and how I wished that she could get something for all the work she had done. I also tried to get her to do my show. She was so broke, she asked that we pay for her gas. But at that time in my career I wasn't making that kind of money, so I couldn't afford to do so.

Dorothy's now in her seventies, and I would still like to have her on my show and do an interview with her before she passes on. She was one of the real pioneers of gospel music. This time I promise to pay for her gas.

This gospel legend was performing back in the 1950s. The fifties was the golden era for gospel music. It was an era when all the great groups like Dorothy's arrived on the scene. There were groups like the Caravans and the Davis Sisters performing back then.

Another great performer I got to meet briefly back then was Willie May Ford Smith. She used to perform at some of the Sunday church programs, and my choir used to sing at some of those events. But our conversations were just a "How are you doing, I enjoy your singing," kind of thing.

I remember that Willie May was a great soloist. I'd always say to myself, *What a voice.* At that time I didn't know anything about her vast contributions to gospel music. About all I knew of Willie May was that she lived in St. Louis, and that her daughter was also a great singer. Much, much later I would get to meet her and learn that she had also worked with Mahalia Jackson when Mahalia was just starting out.

She was definitely a legend. Willie May and Sallie Martin helped Dr. Dorsey when he was trying to popularize gospel music way back in the 1930s. They were the singers for him, the writers of some of his music, and they also sold his sheet music. I didn't know anything about Thomas A. Dorsey, the founder of modern gospel music, who Willie had worked with back in the 1930s, or about other gospel-music pioneers like Sallie Martin, who was also a friend of Dorsey's.

Later on I got to know Willie May quite well. She called me her son. But when I first saw her in St. Louis—it was between 1960 and 1962—it was a time in my life when I was first being introduced to all these performers.

Those were my introductory years. Back then I'd sit in the balcony of the Keil Auditorium and watch some of these legendary gospel groups work. There would be one group after another: the Davis Sisters, the Mighty Clouds of Joy, and James Cleveland, who was called "the King of Gospel." I remember attending some of his early Gospel Music Workshops of America, which were then held in St. Louis.

I remember that the Davis Sisters were just as impressive as Dorothy Love Coats and the Gospel Harmonettes. They were from Philadelphia. And they also sang in these robes. They were hard-singing gospel folk, and I was interested in watching them because I had my own little gospel group. I wanted to see how they did what they did and what their secrets were for attracting such large crowds. But I never did meet any of them or have any conversations with them.

It was a pleasurable spiritual adventure hearing all these people, but at the time I was watching these performers I still wasn't thinking about becoming a professional entertainer. Sure, I knew how to play the keyboard and I had done some singing with the Meister Singers; but above all, I was a teacher. I was convinced that teaching was how I was going to make my living.

After a while, I'd get to recognize some of the same people attending these gospel-music concerts I used to go to. There was this group of people who liked to do the same thing I was doing. One of them was a young woman by the name of Merdean Gales, who is now the co-host of my television show.

When I first met Merdean and her husband, they were the divas of St. Louis church society. When they came into the church everyone stopped talking to stare. She was gorgeous and he was handsome and I just admired them from afar. They were the leaders in the church community at the time.

She is still gorgeous and quite talented. There is little doubt that the popularity of my television program owes a lot to Merdean's efforts as my co-host.

Souls Set Free

At the time I was living in St. Louis, efforts to integrate Nashville had begun. The sit-ins had started in that period, and I watched all that on TV. I would even recognize some of the people they showed on camera.

They would film these disturbances and I saw how the whites would treat the demonstrators—how they would stub them with cigarettes. I felt very bad about what I saw. I had always felt bad about the way blacks were treated in the South.

I had always hoped that whites would come to their senses and change their behavior. A lot of them did. It was good to see white people demonstrating with the blacks and to see Jews—who also know a lot about being oppressed—leading some of the civil-rights marches.

Yet a part of me didn't want to take part in these demonstrations. I admired the protesters, but frankly, I was afraid. Later on, I would take a stand against segregation on a very frightening trip I made to South Africa. But at this time I wasn't going to get involved.

So I watched it all on television. From what I saw, I learned a lot about the realities of the relationships between blacks and whites. I grew a lot from observing what was going on in those critical times that were "the sixties." And, later, as I've already mentioned, I would put my convictions about battling racism into action in the heart of apartheid country.

Dr. Martin Luther King's Assassination, and I'm Off to Jail

Dr. Martin Luther King Jr., Robert Kennedy, Malcolm X, and President Kennedy were assassinated in the 1960s. I remember being in St. Louis and on my way to the house of some friends when Dr. King was killed.

There was a curfew after the assassination of Dr. King, and blacks couldn't be out on the street. So the cops stopped my car about a block away from my friends' house. They made me get out, and spread-eagled me. One cop took the butt of his gun and hit me between my legs and my arms. Then they put me in a paddy wagon. I thought for sure they were going to kill me.

One of the cops growled at me:

"Nigger, don't you know you ain't supposed to be out this time of night? You're supposed to be in. We have a curfew."

"Yes sir. I know that, but I have to see my aunt," I lied. The cops weren't interested in who I was planning to see. So they threw me in the paddy wagon and I went to jail for the first time in my life. It was a horrific experience.

The only thing that made it a bit less horrifying is that there were a lot of us. So when I got into the paddy wagon I saw other people I knew. We arrived at the Metro Jail in downtown St. Louis about eleven or twelve at night.

I remember that they fingerprinted us. Then someone grabbed me by the back of my pants. They put handcuffs on me, and shackles on my feet. Then they took me to this cell with about eighty other men in it. It was a big, open space with a little bathroom in the corner.

I can still remember how bad that cell smelled. I was there for three or four hours. I was scared and I was angry—angry at white people. I couldn't understand why they were so mean and why they would do this to us.

I hoped that one day we would overcome this kind of treatment and get them back for doing this to us. On the other hand, the principal of my school was white and he was a very nice man. He helped to get me out of this situation, and I am deeply grateful for that.

While in the lockup, the cops let me make one phone call. I called my godmother. And she called the principal of my school, who got me out.

When I left the jail I lost some of my anger. I realized there might always be black-and-white issues, but there were some good white people as well as bad white people. The incident turned out to be an embarrassing situation for the police department, because the story of my arrest appeared in the newspapers.

Thinking back to those days, besides recalling the anger I felt at being unjustly arrested, I remember how devastated I was by Dr. Martin Luther King's assassination.

I don't remember exactly where I was when he died. But I do

remember the riots and that I was teaching in a white neighborhood. They didn't riot in the area I was in, but it still was a very difficult time for me—for all blacks.

Especially difficult for me was the experience of being thrown in jail and the way the jailers treated us blacks. I just didn't feel we warranted that kind of treatment. We just happened to be at the wrong place at the wrong time. And what I learned most of all from that experience is that it didn't matter what you did—whether you were a teacher or not. If you were black, you were the enemy.

Sure, it made me feel bitter, but, as I said, not toward every white person. My principal who got me out of jail was white. And my students were white. I wasn't going to try and impede their learning process by being hostile to them.

Back to Nashville

I wanted to go back to Nashville, and had applied for various teaching jobs. But they were almost impossible to find. I wanted to go back because of the good memories I had of my days at Tennessee State University. I also wanted to get my master's degree, which I eventually did—along with a doctorate from Vanderbilt University in Nashville.

I had established a lifestyle there that I loved—especially going to basketball and football games. I also missed all my friends. It was a comfortable lifestyle, and when I moved to St. Louis all of that was left behind me.

In St. Louis, I never got into anything much except for going to church and meeting church people. So I kept sending out job applications to various schools in Nashville.

Finally, one of the schools accepted my application. It would mean making less money, but I really wanted to leave St. Louis because of my lack of social activity there and also because it was such a crime-ridden city. I wanted to get out of there, too, because of the negative experience of having been thrown in jail.

I returned home to Nashville in September 1965. I was only twenty-six years old. I would be teaching fifth grade at an integrated elementary school—the Lakeview Elementary School. The principal was white, and I would be the only black teacher at the school. I was hired to help integrate the school system.

It was a beautiful summer morning when I finally left St. Louis, and never did I expect that I would soon be returning to this city that I so much despised. As I hitched my trailer with all my belongings to the rear of my recently acquired 1959 Chevrolet, I was filled with excitement and anxiety.

I was delighted to be leaving St. Louis, but also kind of anxious about what lay ahead of me. I didn't know what to expect going into an integrated teaching environment. I had always taught in all-black schools or, in St. Louis, a mostly all-white school. I didn't know how I was going to fit in there.

So while I was looking forward to the experience of being in a truly integrated school. I was also curious about how it would all turn out. It turned out that I had no problems. I had a great principal and the other teachers were all supportive. I guess I was blessed, as I always have been for most of my life.

An Opportunity of a Lifetime

I eventually transferred to another elementary school for a change of pace. It was called Head Elementary School and it was located in north Nashville. The students were all black, and I taught there for about a year. I was teaching science and math and helping the teachers develop strategies for teaching.

In the meantime, I had gotten my master's degree in education from Tennessee State University. While I was teaching at Head Elementary School, I had been observed by representatives of the McGraw-Hill textbook company who were operating reading programs in various inner-city schools.

They liked what they saw. I was trying to get my students to realize that learning can be simplified through diligence, discipline, honesty, hard work, and having respect for oneself and others. So McGraw-Hill offered me a job as an educational consultant. They were trying to help inner-city kids learn to read better using a phonetic approach, and they taught me how the system worked.

It was in 1967 that I accepted that job, and that's when real changes began to happen in my life. But there was one catch to that job that nearly gave me a heart attack—I would have to work for the company in their St. Louis office!

But as much as I hated St. Louis I couldn't turn this opportunity down. The money was great and, best of all, I would have a chance to travel to places I never thought I would ever see. The job also gave me a wonderful opportunity to improve my own speaking skills. I became more confident in both my language skills and delivery. I was able to speak in front of large audiences without any embarrassment or awkwardness about the way I spoke.

The job resulted in other profound changes in my life. I always had a salesperson traveling with me, and they were always white. These different salesmen taught me a lot of things about the white man's world I never would have known about.

As a result of my travels with these salesmen, I learned about architecture; I learned about menus and the proper way to order a meal, and about different kinds of foods—all kinds of classy things that I otherwise never would have had an opportunity to learn about.

I remember one evening going into this restaurant with my partner, David, who was from Boston and usually traveled with me. I wanted some veal. And when it arrived it already had parmesan on it. But David requested that the parmesan be brought to the table *after* the meal arrived. It was another lesson in being a sophisticated diner which beforehand I had never really known about.

Also, now—for the first time in my life—I had an expense account. In addition, I was earning enough money to help pay for my mom's new house. It was, all and all, a very incredible, life-changing experience.

Teaching, Again

After a couple of years I got tired of traveling for McGraw-Hill. It was 1974 or 1975, and I was weary of all the traveling and the loneliness.

And somewhere along the line I had fallen in love with a nurse who lived in Nashville. Her name was Jean Davis, and she sang in one of the choirs I used to work with. That was another reason why I wanted to come back home.

There was also a group called the Royal Gospel Singers that I was working with in Nashville. Whenever I could get off on weekends from my job with McGraw-Hill, I would go back to Nashville and sing with them. So besides seeing Jean, I thought about how much fun it would be singing with this group full-time.

I remember once I traveled with this group to Indianapolis. And there was this fantastic choir on the program, headed up by the Reverend Milton Brunson. Listening to them lifted me to another level. They were awesome, inspiring.

Reverend Brunson had put this choir together in Chicago. They had played for a number of years, but weren't really big then—although they were very good. They sang traditional gospel music and had a tremendous number of lead singers within the group. After I heard them sing, I invited them to Nashville to sing at the university. But it really wasn't until 1985 that I got to know Reverend Brunson personally.

In the meantime, I ended up working at an elementary school on the south side of Nashville called the Paul Hamilton Elementary School. I wasn't too happy doing this, because I really wanted to teach on the university level. But I couldn't find work, so I took this teaching job. I think it was 1972 or 1973. I knew I wasn't going to remain there too long as a teacher. I felt that I had grown far beyond that, at the time. But it was a way for me to get back to Nashville.

I taught there for a year, and then I finally got a job teaching reading at Tennessee State University. In the meantime, I began to get involved with two organizations that involved me in the heart and soul of Nashville's black community.

7

Oprah and Project Help

While I was still teaching elementary school, I decided to start an organization that I called Project Help. I was upset with some of the local preachers because they had all these elderly women coming to their churches and I didn't feel they were giving these ladies enough assistance.

These ladies would give all their money to the church and had no money left to get a ride home. And some of these pastors wouldn't even offer to help. I thought that was deplorable. I thought they should have provided for these elderly ladies.

That fall, I had gone to the Reverend James Cleveland's Gospel Music Workshop of America, and saw these mass community choirs that had developed in other parts of the country. Nashville didn't have one, so some of the people at the GMWA asked me if I wanted to organize one of these mass choirs.

I put together this choir and I called it Love Train. There were 350 singers that I recruited from other choirs in the city. We got the name from the O'Jays song, "Love Train." I was proud of this choir. These were just regular people from the community—a lot of them not educated. Some of them were gay and some of them were physically handicapped. But I got them together and involved them in a positive cause.

I decided that we'd do one program a month—the first Sunday

night—and all the money from this concert would go toward funding Project Help. These concerts were jam-packed.

Back in those days Oprah was an anchorwoman on Channel 5 in Nashville, and also doing radio reporting. Oprah had noticed my efforts to help Nashville's elderly population—I had fallen in love with these senior citizens—and I was getting a little celebrity status as a result of Love Train.

Oprah also loved gospel music, so she started coming to my programs. We soon became good friends during that period. She also began coming to my house for Saturday-night parties I used to throw. The house was located right next to one I had built for my godmother, Ms. Childress, so that I could look after her.

Oprah would bring some friends and her then boyfriend. We hit it off very well. I had always wanted to get to know her, even though some people in the community didn't like her because they thought she was phony.

I remember the first time I met her I didn't really think of her as special. She was just another person, so there was no true excitement about meeting her. I was pleased with what she had contributed to the black community. But when I got to know her better, I sensed her ambition. And it's been great to see how she has accomplished what she wanted to do. I could see that the potential was always there, and my instinct about her was right. She certainly has arrived!

Police Story

I used to throw parties at my house in Nashville after Black Expo events. That is, until I got robbed during one of them. It was a Saturday night and my house was full of people—including some of Nashville's top dignitaries. I was having a reception for Ted Lange from *The Love Boat*, and BernNadette Stanis, who played Thelma on *Good Times*. We were all enjoying ourselves when all of a sudden there was this bang on the door.

Someone opened the door and here comes these men with hoods and shotguns. It was horrible. One of these guys says, "Get on the floor, empty your pockets." I couldn't believe this was happening in my home!

So four of these guys ransacked my apartment while all the guests were being accosted and money was being taken from them. I was laying on the floor praying that nobody would get killed.

What these robbers didn't know is that my house had a lower level. My roommate was standing on the landing of the lower level and he could see them through the door. So he was able to get outside and over the fence to my godmother's house and call the police.

The police got there almost immediately. While we were all lying on the floor the police came in. One of these guys was coming up some stairs and this policeman said, "Drop your gun."

Well, he didn't, and the policeman killed him. Then the police were firing at the others. One of these guys ran and jumped through my bedroom window, and the other two jumped out of another window and escaped. They jumped over a fence and got all cut up. The police caught them eventually because they were injured.

Fortunately, none of my guests was seriously hurt. One or two of them were grazed by shells. It was a major story in the Nashville papers because it was at my home and because of the local celebrities who were there. That was the end of my party days in Nashville. It also put a halt in a lot of other social gatherings in the city for a while.

8

The First Black Expo, the Reverend Jesse Jackson, and Some Other Friends

There were a couple of teachers at Nashville's Jenson State University who, when they were students at Vanderbilt University, also located in Nashville, had experienced some abuse because they were black. Their names were Levi Jones, Walter Surce, and Raymond Richardson.

They had seen my work helping the elderly in the community, and wanted to know if I would work with them on this idea they had for a Black Expo. They were putting together a committee of community leaders.

What they wanted to do was increase awareness of all aspects of black culture in Nashville. They thought I had good organizational skills, which I did, because of what I had learned while working with McGraw-Hill. I was teaching at Tennessee State University then, and I agreed to help.

So I helped to develop and organize the first Black Expo, and I was made the president of the organization. It was a wonderful opportunity to expose the contributions of black people in the area.

We held the first Black Expo at Tennessee State University. There were various artists, different kinds of music, exhibits, and local celebrities as guest speakers. It was nicely attended, and successful enough for us to hold it the following year at Nashville's Municipal Auditorium.

We brought in groups like the O'Jays, and television and movie celebrities like Amanda Cole and Ted Lange. We had all these churches show up with banners, and the Reverend Jesse Jackson was the guest speaker.

The first time Reverend Jackson came to speak at the Expo, I didn't really have a chance to talk to him. Later we became good friends. My first impression of him was that he was a strong leader and had a lot to say.

Later on, when I had my television gospel-music show, I had the opportunity to be with him in many situations. There have been many times when he's asked me to do things for him, like help to develop a choir in this or that city or appear on his own television program—which I've done.

Once I even went to Chicago after getting a special telephone call from him. Reverend Jackson wanted me to be part of a meeting with black ministers from around the nation who were trying to lay out a positive agenda for our community.

We still try to get together whenever there is an opportunity. When I see him, I always tell him how much I admire what he does. And I know he admires me, because he gave me an award from Operation Push.

When we talk, it's really just two black men chatting. He's a warm, very regular kind of person. He lets you know that he's a regular kind of person. It's not always business and politics that he's talking about. Most of the time when we get together we talk about people and situations. We're wise enough not to always involve ourselves in rhetoric about what we do.

But his concern about black people always comes out, even if we're talking about music or sports. He's always trying to find solutions to problems affecting our community. And he's always trying to bring these problems to the attention of the country.

I remember a time when Reverend Jackson talked to me about a song that I'd done which he didn't like. There was a lyric in that song about the "battle not being yours, because it is the Lord's." He said to me: "You know, Bobby, the battle is ours." The point he was trying to make was about black power, but I thought it was kind of interesting that he took that stand. I still believe that the battle is the Lord's, but that we're supposed to put into it as much as we can.

I must say that I'm glad to call Reverend Jackson my friend. He can't sing, but he sure is an excellent preacher. I'm proud to know him. He and the Reverend Farrakhan are the two best-known African-American political figures I have had a personal relationship with and have spent a lot of time with.

Another celebrity I got to know briefly when I was doing the Expos was Natalie Cole, who is the daughter of the great star Nat "King" Cole. Columbia Records had sent her over to perform at the show.

Natalie wasn't that well known back then in the 1970s. She sounded a lot like Aretha Franklin, and had a hit record or two. I was a bachelor and had a very nice place, and I'd always invite this attractive young singer over for a reception after her performance.

I remember one evening when Natalie came over—it was her birthday—and John Amos, who was the star of *Good Times*, also was there. I must say that I felt honored to be entertaining stars in my apartment. Although I didn't get to know Natalie all that well, I remember having a very positive impression of her—I still do.

Thinking back, what the Black Expos did was help me develop a good relationship with a lot of people in Nashville and nationally. But then problems began to develop. Some of the organizers couldn't get along with each other. It was a shame. And some of the people in the organization were becoming too political. They were using Black Expo to get themselves into leadership positions on the city council; they had a political agenda for the organization. There were other agendas, also, like one time there was a Communist on our committee and he brought in a Cuban exhibit to the auditorium. He wanted to show the black community how militant he was.

When I discovered all this going on, I began to pull away. I got disappointed and began to lose my desire to participate in any more Black Expos. I wanted to promote the cultural achievements of black people—not get involved in various political agendas.

There was another reason why I left the organization: I didn't like all the jealousy that was beginning to develop in the black community over my accomplishments with the Black Expo. They were making up stories about me stealing money, doing this and doing that. There were even local preachers who began to talk about some of the singers in the Love Train. They didn't like the idea that we had some gay people in the group and some former alcoholics.

I just couldn't understand why the city was being supportive of my efforts, but my own people were not. It really hurt me that I had unwittingly developed so many enemies. By then I had been with Black Expo for about four or five years. They were good years, and I had enjoyed the prestige of being its president. But when it all started to get complicated I didn't really want to participate any further.

Although I left my job as president of Black Expo, the Love Train group kept going until 1976. The Project Help office was running smoothly and we continued to raise money to help the elderly. We had volunteers working as secretaries. We'd feed the poor, pay phone bills for people who couldn't afford it, and even buy medicine for some senior citizens. I was very proud of all the work that Project Help was doing in the community.

When the Black Expo—and, eventually, Project Help—finally came to an end, I didn't have any regrets. I had given the black community my heart and my best and I was ready to move on. I had made some serious contributions to my community, and had stayed with it for quite a while. It was time to do something else. I think it was because of all my exposure in the media and on television, that I now began to think about establishing my own career on television.

The Reverend Al Sharpton's Funny Hair

I'd be remiss to mention Reverend Jackson without briefly mentioning another politically active reverend who is a very dear friend of mine—the Reverend Al Sharpton, who is from New York City. He is someone I got to meet in the 1990s through my television show.

I remember that Reverend Sharpton's office once called me to ask if I would come to New York City to host an event for him. I was flattered. I had always wanted to meet him because he was an anomaly on TV—his hair and everything! It's because of his unusual appearance that I looked at him with a bit of disdain. I'm very much into always looking well-groomed!

But that was before I got to know him. As time went on, I changed my opinion of him. The more I listened to him, the more I realized he wasn't trying to promote himself, as some people have criticized him for doing—he wasn't trying to make himself. I came to believe that he really wanted to do something to help his people—that he was very serious about struggling to help alleviate a lot of the ills of our people.

So when I met him I really regarded him with admiration. I didn't even notice his hair! I was very impressed with him. And his wife is absolutely divine—a very regular person. I once even invited Reverend Sharpton to Nashville to do my show, and he did; he gave a little talk on the show.

I've know Reverend Sharpton for about six or seven years. When we talk on the phone, it's usually about social issues involving black people. We reflect on some of the things he's done in the past, and chat about his future plans. There is always substance to our conversations. Whenever Reverend Sharpton calls me, there is something going on that he wants me to be part of, and I appreciate that.

A Star Is Born

In 1976 I was still teaching reading skills at Tennessee State University, singing with a couple of church choirs, doing some traveling, and trying to maintain the Love Train.

It was because of the Love Train that I got to know this young woman—Nettie Stowers—who had one of these Sunday-morning black-community-affairs programs in Nashville. Her quest was to represent everything that black folk did in the community—she wanted to have a gospel-music presentation, and she loved the Love Train.

Well, it turned out to be an excellent production. We had a set designed and built for it, and the music was great. We enjoyed it, and so did Ms. Stower's assistant, Theresa Hannah.

Theresa came to me and said we should try to get together and see if we could do some kind of regular gospel show. So we did a pilot. I think it was April of 1976 when we first introduced *The Nashville Gospel Music Show.* The station accepted it, and that pilot would later become *Bobby Jones Gospel.*

I was elated. I remember being as excited about the opportunity to get regular exposure for the Love Train on television as I was for myself being the show's host. I just loved the idea, and saw the possibilities of what could be accomplished with this show. I was already hoping that since we were on an NBC affiliate, that the network would love it and broadcast it nationally. I didn't realize at the time that religious programming wasn't something the networks were looking for.

In fact, at that time it was relatively rare to have a black gospel-music show on TV. Gospel was on a serious decline during this period in the 1970s. It was mostly confined to early-morning presentations on local radio.

There were very few—if any—all-gospel-music radio stations back then. And advertising revenues for such shows were small. It wasn't like today, where there is literally an explosion of gospel music and hundreds of radio stations across the country play this format.

So this show was a gamble. I'd even go as far as to say that this gospel TV show might have saved the gospel-music industry, because it helped to keep interest in this type of music alive.

But at the time, I remember being in seventh heaven. *Wow!* I was on television hosting my own gospel-music show. I think they gave us five hundred dollars a week for expenses, and we had a thirteen-week trial period. But as excited as I was, I wasn't overconfident. I didn't quit my job teaching at Tennessee State University.

𝓛ooking back, I guess I didn't fully realize it then, but this was the beginning of another phase of my life. It was my first serious television venture, which would eventually lead me to do something major.

I might add, however, that *The Nashville Gospel Music Show* wasn't my first exposure as host of a television program. A couple of years earlier, in 1973, I had been the co-host of a kids' show on Channel 5 called *Fun City Five*.

A community activist I knew was hired as community coordinator on that station, and he wanted to produce a children's program. He knew about my educational background with McGraw-Hill, so he asked me to audition. I got the job. It was a Saturday-morning program with little games and kids doing different things. I remember that there were five or six regulars on the show and these kids would talk about some news event. We also had puppet characters and segments where kids would learn about science or whatever.

It was only a kids' show, but I remember being very excited about doing it. It was my first big opportunity to be on television. I had done all this work with children through my McGraw-Hill job, so I thought I could put these skills to work in a different medium. The show also was important to me because it was the realization of a fantasy that I had carried with me since those days in Paris, Tennessee, when I bought my first TV set and practiced to be a newscaster.

The program eventually ended, but my television career continued. I wanted it to; I had gotten to enjoy television very much. In fact, I even applied to be a television news reporter on Channel 4 in Chicago because I felt I had the speaking ability to do that. I always had a different kind of thing about language than the people I grew up with. I didn't talk like my peers did, and, as I mentioned earlier, I was ostracized for it. People thought I was trying to be somebody I wasn't because I spoke a little differently than they did.

But I didn't get the job. Although I had control of the language, they turned me down because my look wasn't right for them. I was disappointed, because I had always wanted to be a news anchorman and be able to put my linguistic skills to use.

So I had focused on the Love Train and Black Expo. Then, just a few years later, I was given the opportunity to host my own gospel-music show. It was this opportunity to be on television, in an *important* way—not hosting a kids' show—which I had always known would be coming to me, ever since I was a youngster parked in front of my television set.

I'm not a sorcerer and I'm not a prophet, but I've always had this ability to be able to see certain things in the future. I believe that there are some people that the Lord blesses with this kind of future sight. I'm one of those who believes that he is divinely guided in such a manner.

. . .

One of the first groups I had on my new show was the Williams Brothers. I had met them at one of the James Cleveland workshops, and it was the start of a long friendship. It was at one of those workshops that I had a chance to go backstage and say hello to them. I thought they were a very good quartet. I met one of the brothers, Leonard Williams—he's not with the group right now—and I told him how much I enjoyed their presentation. Later on I would get to know him and the other Williams Brothers much better.

Besides the Williams Brothers, I recall that we brought in as much local talent as we could. John P. Kee did our show during that period, and the Reverend Al Green. Al Green had come from the secular side of music into gospel, so he needed the gospel-music platform that my show offered. Later on, in the 1980s, I got to know Al better when he appeared on my current syndicated program on BET.

The Nashville Gospel Music Show aired at nine A.M. on Sundays, and we turned out to be the program with the highest ratings during that time slot. But I was always thinking about how to improve the show, so I organized the first New Life Singers. I wanted to bring these people in and name them "Bobby Jones and Somebody." I remember discussing what I should call the new group with my godmother. I can still recall sitting in the kitchen with this wonderful woman and talking about names. We finally came up with the name New Life.

I initially chose about nine people plus the keyboard player who was playing for Love Train. Then we brought in other musicians and put this entity together. That was my first New Life group, and they were excellent. In 1982 the New Life Singers would win a Grammy with me, for Best Performance by a Black Contemporary Gospel Group, for our album *Soul Set Free*.

Our Nashville show was on the air for five years—basically with local talent. Then, in 1977 or 1978, I was offered another program on Nashville's Channel 8, which was a public broadcasting station. It was a community-affairs talk show called *Bobby Jones' World*, and it aired for about eight years. I was doing this and my gospel music show both at the same time.

It was through the *Bobby Jones' World* show that I began to meet the major gospel-music stars. It was a magazine-style show, although sometimes we'd have a musical presentation. I also got the opportunity to meet world-renowned authors, entertainers, and national leaders. We would bring in stars like the Jackson Five or Stevie Wonder, and I'd have conversations with them about their lives and careers. We had wine tasters, people from food companies—an array of people.

I learned an awful lot during that period. I didn't make much money from the show, but I was dedicated to it and we always got good ratings. I also won several awards for that program, including the Gabriel Award in 1980. That award was for a black gospel opera that I wrote and produced in Venice, Italy. It was called *Make a Joyful Noise* and it eventually aired on the Public Broadcasting System.

Meeting Maya Angelou

What can I say about Maya Angelou? I first met her between 1976 and 1977 when I was teaching at Tennessee State University, producing two television shows, and working on my doctorate in education at Vanderbilt University—all at the same time!

Maya was the first big celebrity that I ever had a chance to get to know personally. I met her when Dr. Ruby Martin, the lady who hired me at the university, invited Maya to be a guest speaker at one of our functions. It was during Maya's presentation that I kind of locked in to her. I loved what she was saying, and I think she singled me out in the crowd. Afterward, we had a little function at a hotel, and Dr. Martin introduced me to her.

I told Maya that I would take her to the airport the following morning, and on that drive we had a chance to chat. She really liked me. I gave her an album—our first album—and not too long afterward she called me and asked if I would come to Los Angeles to do a benefit for her aunt's church.

I packed up the people who worked with me and rented a bus— she didn't pay us for transportation, but only provided for the hotel. She didn't even mention how we would get there, and I didn't bring it up. When I think back on it, it really was not in order for her to ask me to bring all these people to California to do a concert, and not mention a thing about transportation.

So we ended up paying for the trip ourselves, and we checked in to a hotel. Despite all that, I was on cloud nine because I was doing something for Maya Angelou, the great African-American poet and writer.

One evening we went to her residence. She had a cookout for us. She had Hollywood people there, and the president of Universal Studios. I felt that I was getting ready for a great ride, and that turned out to be true.

It was through Maya's influence that I ended up being in a movie. It was a 1982 NBC-TV *Movie of the Week* called "Sister, Sister," and starred Diahann Carroll, Paul Winfield, Irene Cara, and Rosalind Cash. Maya had written that movie, and she called me and asked me to come to Alabama, where it was being filmed; there was a scene in the church with a choir, and the choir they were using was inadequate. So I jumped into the van with my New Life Singers, and we were off to Montgomery, Alabama, to do a movie. When I found out who the stars were in the movie, boy, was I impressed! And I even got a chance to do the opening line in the movie.

I remember going over to Diahann Carroll's apartment and teaching her a couple of the songs we were going to do in the movie. Imagine that! What a great experience that was. Diahann was easy to teach. I was there with the choir, and she would join in and sing with us. And then she asked us to sing for her, and really appreciated it. I had a very cordial relationship with her. She's a very warm person. There were times during the filming when we got tired. Diahann would come over and say things to us that would inspire us. I liked her very, very much.

We even made some money doing this movie. This experience with Maya Angelou will always be an important part of my life. And that movie is still being shown on TV. They keep rerunning it.

Ever since that time, I've visited Maya in different places. We've even performed in her church a couple of times. I remember once that I was invited to her birthday party, but I was giving a concert at the same time. It was on a Saturday afternoon, and I had decided that I was going to catch a plane and make her party, and then catch another plane and do my concert that evening.

Well, I missed the plane by three or four minutes and didn't make the party. I was upset, because I had wanted to be with her; I also missed one of the best birthday parties of the year, which was written up in *Gent* magazine.

Since then, I've been invited to her home many times, and she's been at my house in the Green Hills area of Brentwood many times. In fact, I have some shoes that belong to her that she left behind the last time she stayed over here.

To me, Maya is an inspiration. She has a special insight into the human condition and about society in general. She is a fountain of information and has a historic perspective on so many things that apply to black culture. It's really a blessing to be in her presence and listen to her speak.

Taken by a Con Man

It was during the time I met Maya Angelou that I experienced the other side of the coin. I had this bad experience with a guy I can only describe as a sophisticated con man.

As I said, it was a period of my life when I doing three or more things at the same time—teaching, singing, television work. I was even at the point of thinking that I had too much going on and that maybe

I should give some of it up. But I was always a hard worker. And I kind of liked the fact that so many of my students knew me from television and appreciated being in my class. At this time, the New Life Singers were starting to do well.

Luck was with me when I was approached by a man named T. B. Boyd, who was then president of the National Baptist Convention. He was a wonderful and generous man who liked our work and put together a deal with Benson Records. As a result, in 1976 we recorded our first album with that label, called *Sooner or Later*.

It was an interesting experience. Now, in addition to everything else I was doing, I found myself traveling on weekends to different concert dates. On some of these trips our group earned only fifty dollars for gas. Eventually we got to the point where we would charge $250 to perform, and we would divide that little amount of money among the singers and the musicians.

There were so many relationships developed, that I sometimes lost track. But most of all, it was lots of fun to be on the road even if there was no money to be made back in those days. I still have a lot of fond memories of those days traveling with the New Life Singers. I remember the van we traveled in had little sleeper beds in it, and would seat about eighteen people. We would pack all of our music equipment into the van, so some of us had to sit on the floor—it's a good thing the van had carpeting! We managed to go around the country in that van, and to this day I don't know how we managed, with as many people and luggage and equipment we had packed in there.

I also remember that the women in the group would always be chiding each other about various things. They were such aggressive women that I didn't know how to control them. One of my girls, Hilda, she was mean and she was mischievous. And she would always poke fun at the one white girl in the group. Then there was another girl who kept trying to upset one of my singers whose husband was part of the group. She kept telling the poor woman that her husband was being pursued by one of the other girls.

One time, when we had gone to do a television program in Johnson City, Tennessee, on the way back we got stuck in a snowstorm. There we were in a town called Coolow, Tennessee, and we had to find a hotel room. There were ten of us, and only one room was available. So all ten of us had to stay in that room. I think there were four guys and six women. But it ended up being a lot of fun because we just slept all over the floor. We had to stay there a couple of days.

We had to clean our clothes in the sink, and the women would wash for us. One of the women who was washing clothes was Regina McCrary, who went on to sing with Stevie Wonder. Now she's back with my New Life Singing Aggregation.

As the New Life Singers became more successful, the group grew larger. Much of its success was due to Gary Jones, my music director, who is an astute writer, arranger, and musician. And another man I must credit is Donald Watkins. He was also instrumental in helping me with my New Life Singers.

One day a young man joined our organization. He said he had all kinds of promotional skills. He offered me a lot of hope that I would become a national celebrity. I didn't know at the time that he really didn't know what he was doing—and, worse, that he was a con man. This man said he would be able to promote me and the New Life Singers for a fee of fifteen thousand dollars. So I went and borrowed the money—and that was a lot of money at that time—from T. B. Boyd.

This con artist said our group would become a major fund-raiser for sickle-cell anemia, and that various companies would give us donations. He painted a beautiful picture. He took the fifteen thousand dollars, and then it became more thousands of dollars that he said he needed to promote us. I had even bought beautiful uniforms for the women in the group, and tuxedos for the guys. I thought we were all really on the way. We were, but never as quickly as this con man who eventually disappeared had promised us.

10

Barbara Mandrell Defies the Rules

It was after this experience with the con man that I met Barbara
Mandrell, a woman who is still one of my best friends in life. I had
just established an even larger singing entity called the New Life Ensemble, and they were appearing with me on my television program.

I didn't know it, but Barbara was one of the biggest fans of our
show. She used to watch our program regularly—especially when we
had a performer on who she absolutely adored, Andrae Crouch.

It was in 1979 that I finally got to meet Barbara. I was delighted
that she had taken an interest in me and my ensemble. I really couldn't
believe it when she walked into my studio wearing this beautiful black
top and white chiffon bottom. She was calling me by my first name
and talking with us and singing with us—it was quite a highlight for
me. Then, a year later, she called and asked me to consider going with
her to Las Vegas where she was doing her first revue.

Needless to say, I was just beside myself to go there. It wasn't the
gambling that attracted me to that city, but the shows, and the show-
business people I could see there, doing their acts.

I remember that Barbara invited me to her home and showed me
the wardrobe that the girls in the ensemble would wear. I was as impressed by that as much as I was to learn that she had a dress designer,
a set designer, a musical director, and dancers all involved in her show.

Thinking back, I can say quite honestly that meeting Barbara

Mandrell was heaven on earth. And it's the way I still feel about her today. She is the dream of my life. In all these years, we have never had a moment of not getting along. Barbara has always showed me love and kindness, and I respond to that. She did so much for my ego, being this country-music woman who was willing to accept a black guy.

You know, basically speaking, how country-music people are when it comes to black folk. It's typical of how a lot of white America feels toward blacks, and country-music fans just tend to follow suit.

Barbara defied all the rules when it came to working with somebody like me. I was a bit nervous about playing before an all-white country-music audience, but I felt slightly protected working with her.

Still, I never knew what to expect. But to my relief, her fans were nice to us. We didn't get any jeers or anything from the people in the audience. If we had, I would have just seen it as a way of life in certain parts of this country, and continued with my life and career.

It was the same thing working with Wayne Newton, Ricky Skaggs, and Ronnie Milsap. We were treated well by the stars and there was no negative input from the audiences.

About Barbara, I can never say enough. She absolutely loves all people, and gospel music. In fact, she grew up listening to gospel music. On Sundays, her parents used to invite people over to their home for gospel singalongs.

That first time when I met Barbara we were in the studio recording an album called *There's Hope for This World*. It was on the Nashboro-Creed label. The album didn't do great, but it didn't do too badly, either. Barbara sat in on some of the recording sessions.

From the start I realized what a nice person she was. She always treated me and my singers with dignity and respect. And she developed warm relationships with some of the women in our group. We would even show up at her home for dinner.

Barbara was helpful in getting us some dates at fairs, and she even got us on an NBC special starring Frankie Avalon that was celebrating two-hundred years of American music. Whenever she would have an opportunity to do so, she would bring us into her environment.

Even now, I'm in close touch with her. Not only is she a special lady, but I receive the same kind of treatment from her husband and children. When she recently had her wedding-anniversary party at her Nashville home, I was invited to it. And she has appeared on my TV show.

So, as I said, when Barbara invited us to perform with her in Las Vegas, we went and I opened for her. By this time I had switched record labels. I had moved from Benson Records to Word Records, which was a major Christian record company. We did two albums with Word—both of them were mostly "contemporary Christian" versions of gospel songs.

When I did my album with Word—*Soul Set Free,* which was recorded in 1982—I thought that they would be happy that Barbara Mandrell was working with me. At first they were. Then they reversed themselves. Because they were a Christian record company, they didn't like the fact that a black man and a white woman were working together in a show of the type we were doing in Vegas. So they didn't promote my first album that featured Barbara on it.

The record-company executives must have been shocked when one of the songs from that album—"I'm So Glad I'm Standing Here Today"—was nominated for a Grammy, and that our second album together, *Come Together,* went on to win a Grammy in 1984 for Best Vocal Duo for a Soul Gospel Performance. They didn't even bother to support the Grammy Award that I won with Barbara. But while I felt let down by my record company, that never was the case with Barbara, who has always remained true-blue.

11

Guided by Spirit

The St. Louis and Nashville years were a time of tremendous growth for me. I had come a long way from being that shy kid who lived in a little house on the hill in Henry County. I was well-educated, teaching, had earned my master's degree, and was working on my doctorate. At the same time, I was also becoming something of a local television celebrity in Nashville.

Of course, none of this could have ever happened without God's blessing. It was God's spirit that led me on my course in life—especially my opportunity to spread the Word of God through gospel music. And because I am a religious person, let me briefly tell you what my spiritual beliefs and strengths are.

I believe that I am guided by an outer spirit—I have always thought that even as a small child. As a child, I didn't know what it was or how to call it, but I felt there was some kind of uniqueness that the Lord had put me here for. I'm sure a lot of people feel that way about themselves—I certainly hope they do. So my quest has always been to find out what it was I was supposed to do, and do it. And I believe that's what I'm doing.

I feel there should be no fear when you have a relationship with God and come to an understanding that He is always with you—that His presence is always with you. Once you understand that, there's a spiritual safety zone that you can rest in.

When I pray, I pray to continue to establish the relationship I have with the Lord. I pray for wisdom, direction, and to feel the energy from Him that gives me the opportunities to do what I can do and be of service to His Kingdom.

I don't have any specific time when I pray. I pray whenever I think about it, in any situation where I feel that I need to. So it's not like I wake up every morning and start a prayer at ten or eleven o'clock. But I'm forever mindful of God's presence and grateful for the blessings that the Lord has bestowed upon me. That's a given in my life.

I'm also not a regular churchgoer. That's because of the busy schedule I keep and the hours I work. Sometimes on weekends I have to travel, and I get back to the city on Sunday morning; then I try to make the church service. When I'm here in the city, I always go to church.

Gray Hair, My Beautiful Home, and Bigots

When I look in the mirror I don't see myself as a major celebrity. I know that a lot of people know who I am and a lot of people respond to what I do and appreciate the fact that I'm able to bring the gospel to TV. But there are several other little career steps I need to take to feel I'm a *true* celebrity. I'm certainly very happy about what I do and how I do it, and it may very well be that the Lord feels He can better use me at the exact level that I am at now. But I have ambitions to do even better—not that I want to argue with God's plans for me.

I'm also quite aware of my age—that as of this writing, I am sixty years old. But I'm not like many people who are always worrying about their age. I don't have any fears of death or illness because of my age. I still see myself as young and vital. And I feel blessed. God has always watched over me, even when I've been in some dangerous situations.

So I don't see myself resigning from any of the things I do at this point. In fact, I'm just starting. Every day I'm anxious to get started so I can be sure to accomplish what I need to accomplish. That's why I

work all the time. Work is a never-ending situation with me. I'm someone who enjoys the work he does, and works very hard to make sure
that it is done correctly.

There's always something to do—mail to answer, shows to produce,
phone calls to return, trips to prepare for, books like this one to write,
and records to record. It goes on and on.

But I also like to relax when I can. Although I'm not the kind of
guy who can sit around a pool all day, I do like watching television
news programs and informational shows. I also love going to Las Vegas. It's a place I can go to and not be recognized—just mix with the
people there. I don't care for the gambling aspect of it, but it's just
fun to be there and go to the shows. I enjoy taking a break from the
spotlight.

When I wake up in the morning, I don't concentrate in a heavy,
existential manner about who I see reflected in the mirror. I know it's
me. I see a face that I've been looking at for the past sixty years. I look
at that face carefully only to see if I need a shave or not. I look at my
teeth and my hair to see if I'm getting any grayer. I always examine
myself to make sure I look appropriately groomed, and I'm usually very
pleased with what I see. I like myself. I feel good about myself because
I feel that I'm making a contribution to this world.

I also thank God for allowing me to wake up in this beautiful red
brick Italian-style house on property that Amy Grant's grandmother
used to own—it was once a farm. As a black man, I never dreamed
about living in a mostly all-white suburban community like Greenhills,
in a house designed by Michael Kickerillo.

My home is extraordinary. It's a sprawling refuge that's filled with
paintings I've collected from around the world, sculpture, African art
and masks, and many plaques and trophies I've been awarded over the
years. There are lots of plants, a white baby-grand piano, two white
couches, a colossal glass-wall room divider, and a kitchen that looks out
to my lovely patio. There's even a media room with a theater-size TV
screen. My house also has duel fireplaces and a two-car garage. One

of my cars is a little red Porche Boxter. Yes, I like grandeur, and this house expresses that.

I use one of the rooms in my house as my office, and it is filled with computers, a fax machine that never stops ringing, and editing equipment so that I can work on my show in the comfort of my home.

I'm not lonely, even though at this time I'm living apart from my mate. In fact, I'm very happy. I'm happy to have lived as long as I have, and that I maintain an individual lifestyle where I can make myself happy. I've always had good friends to share my space with me, so I've never really been alone.

I can't afford to be lonely or go into a state of mind that would cause me to be less effective in my job. You have to take care of every facet of your life—including feelings of loneliness or sadness—so that you can be effective in what you do.

In terms of insecurity, none of us is perfect. There are a lot of things I'm insecure about—first of all, about my performance as a singer. I realize the limits of my vocal singing ability. Although I know my performances are perfectly acceptable, if I'm doing a show with other well-known artists who really know how to get a house rocking, I can get a little nervous about my own presentation and its limitations.

Sometimes I have insecurities about my television show—how I'm going to maintain myself if I decide to retire. I haven't found anyone to mentor who could take over the show and continue, what Bobby Jones has brought to the gospel-music industry. I would love for this person to be one of my family members, but their energies are channeled in other directions. I do want to see this ministry continue, however, and I know that in due time someone will appear that I can mentor. I have the utmost faith in that.

And believe it or not, I'm still very shy; I still suffer from self-esteem problems—probably because of my experiences with my father when I was very young. At the same time, it causes me to do what I do. Trying to overcome that shyness has always given me a drive to succeed. I guess I'm still trying to prove myself. I've always been out to prove a point that I am not what my father used to say I was—lazy and worthless.

As far as regrets go, my major regret is—even though I've won a Grammy and other musical awards—I've not yet had a hit gospel album or CD that I consider a *truly* top-of-the-line success. I regret that I haven't accomplished that yet; otherwise I believe everything in my life is in divine order.

I also listen to a lot of music. I'm not much into rap music, although there is some rap that I can understand. And I like listening to blues and popular music as well. I also enjoy some country-music songs. As far as reading goes, I love books. I read a lot of nonfiction—educational materials, journals, books that provide me with information. And whenever I travel on a plane, I always bring a book along to read. I always read a lot when I'm traveling.

Besides gospel music, I also like classical music. I enjoy going to an occasional symphony performance or to the opera. I guess you could say that my musical tastes are flexible. But when it comes to performing, gospel music is my true love.

As you already know, I'm not a big consumer of alcohol, but I do drink socially. Drugs, I never have touched. And I'm always for the underdog, because I have been there. I very much enjoy helping people who are somehow disadvantaged to be the best that they can be.

Sometimes I'm misunderstood because of my desire to help the underdog. When I started my first choir—the Love Train—I had all kinds of people from the Nashville community participating in it: there were deformed people, gays, straights, rejects, you name it. It didn't make any difference to me who they were, as long as they could sing. I embraced them all. So naturally it created a reaction in the community: "Oh, that Love Train."

But it didn't matter to me what my critics said. I wanted these disadvantaged people to have a sense of worth. I wanted them to feel they were part of something that would make them feel good about themselves. I knew what they were, but I also knew who I was; I had been discriminated against by my family when I was young.

I remember that there was a girl in New Life by the name of Bonnie. She was short and dark-skinned, and could holler and sing. She was raised in the housing projects, and I became her tutor. And I said to her one day: "I'm going to put you on TV because I want you to be the one to encourage other black girls who live in south Nashville. I want you to say, 'Look at Bonnie. Look what I've gotten to do. You can do the same thing.' "

I was the Pied Piper—I wanted to show what these underdogs had to offer. That was the energy behind all of that. And I was so disappointed that so many people missed the point.

*B*esides trying to help people, and encouraging them to succeed, I always try to encourage people to take care of their health. That's what I try to do for myself as well—take care of my health.

It's the most important factor in my life. I may not be doing it one hundred percent, but I'm headed in the right direction. I walk at least three times a week—a mile or two—or whenever I have the time. I played tennis regularly until last year, and I still love to play a little basketball.

But most of what I do is calisthenics and walking. Every morning I do fifteen minutes of bends, lifts, and stretches. I also run in place. I think it essential that we keep our bodies in good condition.

So I subscribe to wellness, and I'm concerned about my diet. I've been that way for a long time. I try not to eat too much red meat, and I use herbs occasionally to cleanse my colon. I'm very health-conscious.

Sometimes, though, I think I'm not getting the right amount of sleep. That's because I usually stay up until one-thirty or two in the morning, and get up around nine. Like I said, I'm not one hundred percent perfect . . . yet.

Things I really don't like include religious people who are judgmental of others, anyone who mistreats their parents, and people who dislike people because of their color or race or ethnicity. That's really distasteful to me and I don't like to be in that kind of company.

I like to be with people who see life as it really is—an opportunity for all of us to exist in this world without infringing negatively on anyone else's life. It would all be so simple if we just lived our own lives and left other people alone to do what they want to do.

It's really very simple. I don't bother you, and you don't bother me. If you wear white and you like that, fine. That's none of my business what you like to wear. If you eat this or that, fine.

But if I can be of help to you by telling you not to eat something because it may cause you health problems, I will try to do so. Whether you accept my advice or not, I'm not going to get all blown-out over it. I'll just feel good about myself knowing that I tried.

And, lastly, I don't argue and I don't fight. It's a waste of time. That's probably one of the reasons it took me so long to get into a relationship with a permanent mate—it had a lot to do with my upbringing and the explosive atmosphere that often prevailed in our household when I was a youngster.

A Visit to the Holy Land

In the late 1970s I got the opportunity to visit Israel for the first time as a guest of the Gospel Music Association. I took along six of the New Life Singers—one girl, four guys, and a piano player.

I got to meet the mayor of Jerusalem, and his niece was our guide. Our first performance was at a Jewish settlement, a kibbutz. These Israelis were polite to us and they sang and danced with us. They liked the more traditional gospel songs most of all. They weren't uncomfortable with us. They knew why we were there and that we weren't trying to convert them. Then we visited the Knesset—the Israeli parliament—and we performed at the Jerusalem Theatre.

Everywhere we performed, people responded to gospel music. We played in a park in downtown Jerusalem, and five minutes before we started there was nobody there. By five o'clock the park was totally packed. We performed with a broken-down piano, but the people went crazy over us. It was a wonderful experience.

The best thing about going to Israel was how it helped me develop a closer relationship to my spiritual heritage. Here we were walking through places that I'd only read about in the Bible. We went to Calvary, the Mount of the Beatitudes, and other sites where Jesus and his disciples left their mark. Sometimes it didn't seem real that these places could still exist.

All Christians should make this journey. Going to the Holy Land, for a Christian, is next to going to heaven—it's the place where Jesus walked and did His miracles. I've been to Israel several times since then, but this first visit was like a fantasy. What a thrill for me and the people with me.

I also wanted to see the topography of the land and how the people lived, what they ate, and what the areas were like today where Jesus lived. And we did a lot of that.

Besides seeing what the land looked like, we got to see tanks and ammunition bins alongside the road from Jerusalem to Tel Aviv—reminders of the wars with Arabs.

A bit of excitement took place while we were crossing the Sea of Galilee. One of the women on the tour was a little mentally unbalanced. She kept telling us that we weren't going to make it back to America; but she was the one who almost didn't make it back. As we got to the middle of the sea, this woman suddenly jumped into the water. Two of my singers saw her and shouted, "She jumped, she jumped into the sea!" We looked out and there she was, thrashing about in the middle of the Galilee. Everybody panicked and the boat made a turn. The crew was able to get her out before she went under.

Otherwise, it was an inspiring trip. I remember, before leaving Israel, looking out my hotel window where I could see the rolling hills of Jerusalem, and thinking about the future of this land. I wondered how, with all its enemies, it could be preserved from the dangers that face it.

A Record Flops

Our first album was with Benson Records in 1976. It was called *Sooner or Later,* and it didn't do well, either sooner or later. It was only promoted in the local marketplace. I still thought we were growing artistically—especially when I switched labels to Word Records. There had been a couple of albums in between, on labels like Nashboro-Creed and CBS International. Nothing much came of those, either. But Word was a major label. And even if the record company wasn't too crazy about *Soul Set Free* because of their religious sensibilities, I felt that being on that label was good for my singing career.

I was excited about taking the photo for the cover and participating in the whole process. I wrote three or four songs on that project. The album got some play, but there wasn't a tremendous amount of sales. I was terribly disappointed. I'd been disappointed with all my album sales, so far.

I thought, because we were on TV, that albums we recorded would really sell well. I didn't realize sometimes that can be a hindrance; sometimes being both a television personality and a recording artist just doesn't work. People like to place you in one category or another.

Soul Set Free was a special album but done in a "contemporary Christian" music style. The funny thing was, when we'd go to a Christian venue to perform, the people in the audience got more excited about the real gospel tunes we sang—not their "contemporary Christian" versions.

I believe that's what kind of geared me back to doing gospel music. Because that's what generated all the excitement. At the end of each of our shows with Barbara Mandrell in Las Vegas, we'd do some hard-driving gospel tunes. We'd do a gospel number by ourselves, and then two gospel numbers with Barbara. And those numbers always turned out to be the most exciting parts of the show.

12

Betrayed

Something happened to me in early 1980 that continues to disturb me even to this very day. It was the worst time of my TV experience, and something I have still not completely gotten over.

I was in New York City at the time to receive the Gabriel Award for my PBS-TV special, *Make a Joyful Noise*. Not only did I write a part of that opera, but I acted and sang in the production—I played a minister helping a woman reach a particular pinnacle in her singing career.

It was an exciting moment for me, to be receiving this award. This was the first black gospel-music opera, and it was considered good enough to also win an International Film Festival Award.

That resulted in a trip to Venice, Italy, to receive the honor. But all my excitement would soon turn to deep sadness. Unbeknownst to me, back in Nashville, Theresa Hannah and Tommy Lewis, my co-producers on *The Nashville Gospel Music Show*, had gotten together behind my back and decided that I had too much authority and power on the show.

They wanted more input, so they had an attorney draw up a new contractual agreement. The only way I learned about all this was because there was an article in one of the daily papers. Theresa and Tommy were quoted as saying that I took everything away from them and that they had no say in anything having to do with the show. They were quoted as saying that while they were interested in doing community-oriented shows, I was more interested in producing white gospel music instead of black gospel music. Needless to say, I was shocked. I was also disappointed and heartbroken at this betrayal.

I refused to meet with their attorney. And things got worse. While I was in New York City and then Europe, they called all their people together and got Channel 4 to dismiss me from a show that I had started.

When I found out, it nearly killed me. I never thought that could be done, because *I was the show*! I didn't think they had anything of value to add to a gospel show. But they had manipulated the television station and gotten control of something that I had started and developed.

So we separated. And if it were not for the efforts of some local citizens who had worked with me at Black Expo, I might have permanently lost my job at Channel 4. Friends went to bat for me with the owners of the station.

One of those people was a young black attorney by the name of Richard Manson. Not only is he now my manager, and my best friend to this very day, but anyone who knows CeCe Winans should know that Richard is the manager of this incredibly talented artist as well.

So what happened is that Channel 4 agreed to air two gospel-music shows. And I renamed my show *Bobby Jones Gospel*. I figured that if Phil Donahue and all these other white men could have a show with their names on it, we needed a show with a black man's name on it. I said, I'm going to be bold and do it. My show ran at seven A.M., and theirs at nine A.M. Looking back, not only was the name change for my show significant, but good luck came from it.

I was also able to rebroadcast my show on a then small cable station—Black Entertainment Television, which was owned by a man named Bob Johnson. I signed on as executive producer and host. As a result of all this controversy, I was now being seen on two television stations.

Eventually I left Channel 4, and they made no effort to keep me there. Not many people around the country have heard of Nashville's Channel 4, but more than five million people across the nation watch me each week on the BET network, which has become one of the giants of the cable television industry.

Today I realize that this in another example of how I always have been divinely guided. How every time I've stumbled and not known what to do, another door has opened. After I left Channel 4, not only was my show now being seen on BET, which changed the format from a half hour of gospel music to a full hour, and gave the show better production values, but Nashville's Channel 8, a public broadcasting station, also picked up the program. It just kept getting better and better.

I felt I was betrayed by two people who I thought were my friends. This was probably one of the most depressing periods of my life. I had almost lost all my dreams because of these two people. It was even more distressing because it divided the black community, and left me with a bitter taste toward many people in Nashville.

I became upset that a lot of people in my community whom I had thought were my friends, as well as some of my New Life Singers, rallied toward my opponents at *The Nashville Gospel Music Show*. I was very disturbed by that. It was hard for me to accept that after all the years of public service I had given Nashville's black community, that some people viewed me as the enemy. There were moments back then when the bitterness I felt almost made me want to hang up my hat and leave Nashville. But I didn't.

Instead, I decided to drop out of doing any more activities that were of service to my community. As much as I had done over the years to help them, they should have shown me the same kind of support when I was under attack. But that didn't happen.

If there was any refuge for me, it was the university where I was still teaching. That was a good, stable place for me, and my colleagues were supportive. It helped me get through a very difficult time in my life.

There has never been a better friend to me than Tennessee State University, and nowadays I do everything I can to financially support the university because of its years of loyalty to me.

Earning My Doctorate Degree

It was in 1980 that I finally completed my doctorate at Vanderbilt University. I had taken a temporary leave of absence from teaching at Tennessee State University to complete that higher degree in education. In the meantime, I had continued to work on my television productions and also found some time do a little traveling around the country. It was a very proud moment for me.

I was thirty-nine years old, and not only the first person in the gospel-music industry to have a popular nationally-syndicated television show, but I believe I was also the first gospel-music artist to earn a doctorate degree.

A Spaced-Out Al Green Performs

My work in the gospel-music arena continued to escalate. The BET program was growing in popularity. We were even working on a new idea for the station—a twenty-four-hour, all-gospel network.

One of the stars appearing on my show who most excited me was Al Green. When I announced that he would be on, we suddenly had a studio full of his fans.

Al had an uncanny way of delivering his music—a style and tone that really got his fans involved in his messages. I had a lot of admiration for his skills and I was appreciative that he had agreed to do my show.

I remember being really surprised at his demeanor when he arrived at the studio. He seemed spaced-out and was difficult to talk to because he was wearing these dark glasses and looking here and there and everywhere.

We really didn't even get much of a chance to talk. He arrived just before the show and left right after his performance. But it didn't spoil his performance. That was one evening to remember. I was impressed with him because I loved the "Back Up This Train" song that he did. I was also a little embarrassed for him because of his behavior.

He was proclaiming himself a minister at the time, which a lot of people doubted was authentic. I don't remember if I had any specific thoughts on that matter one way or another; even if I did, I would have kept them private.

The fact that a superstar like Al Green would come to participate on my program was a great lift for me. I needed that because I was trying to prove a point now that it was entirely my show. I was still feeling the effects of being betrayed—the coup that Tommy and Theresa had pulled on me at Channel 4. It also gave me a great lift when Barbara Mandrell did my new show the same year—1980.

All of these artists appearing on my BET program during that period gave me a way to say to Channel 4, *Look at what you missed because you didn't keep me.*

With the success of my new show, plans under way to expand it, and having earned my doctorate, I was beginning to feel a lot better about things. It was a very exciting experience.

Shy Edwin Hawkins

It was, of all places, Holland that I got to meet Edwin Hawkins of the famous gospel-music singing family; I was on tour there at the time with the Gospel Music Association. We had a chance to talk about what was happening at that particular time in the gospel-music industry, about the particular festival we were attending, and what he planned to do in the future.

I told him how impressed I was by the profound Hawkins sound, and how happy I was about the group's popularity. I also learned a couple of things about him—that Edwin was single and how he still stung from the insults he had received over his performance of "Oh, Happy Days."

Many ministers and other gospel-music lovers were offended that he had popularized a gospel-music song that was being played on secular radio stations. So they put him through hell and nearly caused Edwin to suffer a mental breakdown.

They also bashed him for playing Las Vegas. He didn't go into all of this too much. He was in Holland to enjoy himself and to spread his musical ministry. We ended up singing "Oh, Happy Days" together, and the Europeans went crazy over that. It was my way of saying that I supported him. I knew the crowds would respond to that.

In his personal life, Edwin is a shy person. He is a great dresser and loves interior design. In traveling with him, I learned that he was very selective about what he eats. I also discovered that he's a devout Pentecostal, which is a very disciplined religion. He has always been active in that church.

Despite his talent and great stage presence, he is a subtle, quiet-natured type of a guy who doesn't involve himself in much outside of church activities. At one time we had a very close relationship—he was over to my house many times—but I haven't seen him for a couple of years.

I remember once going to one of his Edwin Hawkins Seminars. He had asked me to host his Saturday-night extravaganza. The rest of the Hawkins family was there and, although I was awed by them, I found them a little different in their personalities than I had expected. It was as if they weren't sure how people perceived them, so they were a little standoffish. They made me feel as if I was intruding into their space. Edwin has that same kind of spirit. I think it has to do with shyness, though, rather than feeling like he is something grand.

I remember another time I had met members of the Hawkins family—this was 1976—and I had just recorded my first album, *Sooner or Later,* on the Benson label. In my youthful enthusiasm, I thought it was fabulous like their albums were. So I invited them to my home for a reception and to hear what I had recorded. Well, although I thought I was on the high end, I quickly got put in my place. I remember playing the album and they just laughed in my face. I was secretly so upset, but I didn't say anything.

Tramaine, Walter Hawkins' wife, has a different kind of personality than the rest of the family. She is more forward and pleasant and eager to create conversations. I think I became closer to her than I did to other members of that family.

But after I got to know Edwin better, our relationship improved. We had so many things in common that our friendship developed into a first-class one. I like the fact that he is into interior design, because so am I. And he pays as much attention to his clothes as I do. What we both really have in common is our love of gospel music.

Land of Windmills and Cheese Factories

I never thought that Holland, a land of windmills and cheese factories, would have so many black people living there. It was a pleasant surprise.

Joe Mascheo, one of the officers of the Gospel Music Association who had invited me to go to Israel to represent the group, also gave me the opportunity in 1981 to see the Netherlands for the very first time.

A Dutch minister by the name of John Maasbach was our host. One-third of his church was black. They were from Surinam, which is on the northeastern coast of South America. It's a small country that was once colonized by the Dutch, so many of their citizens ended up relocating to the mainland. By the time Surinam gained its independence from Holland, that little country had been stripped of its wealth by the Dutch. So many Surinamese remained in Holland in order to find work.

There are also a lot Indonesians and other Asians who live in Holland, and many of them also were part of John's church. So Holland is not as white as many Americans might imagine it to be—which is why I was surprised to find that many of the Dutch had the same attitudes toward the Surinese and the Indonesians as many Americans have toward blacks. The Dutch called them "shiftless," and "lazy," and criticized them for wanting to live off the state and get welfare.

It just reiterated the same point over again: If you are white you tend to have the same belief system toward people of color no matter what the country is. Of course there are many exceptions, like the Maasbach family. They were fun to be with and I developed a good relationship with all of them. John Maasbach had seven children, and over the years most of them have come to visit me here in Nashville.

The Williams Brothers

I had met the Williams Brothers on and off over the years during concerts and other public appearances—mostly in the 1980s. They were always a high-energy, great ministry-type organization with good singing. They're a very handsome looking group—friendly, warm—and people love them.

Later on, I developed a closer personal relationship with three of the brothers—Melvin, Leonard, and Douglas. I've known Doug now for about fifteen years. He is a wonderful support to Melvin.

I rate Doug highly as an artist, who would be as successful singing on his own as he is with his group. The times that we've talked, I've been impressed with the way he is involved with his own record label, and especially his involvement in the Christian experience. All you need to do is listen to the lyrics of the songs he's written—they're all filled with personal testimonies—and you'll get a good idea of his strong relationship with Christ and what the Lord has done to help him through many distressing situations.

I remember that whenever I was with the brothers, we'd always have conversations about their travels and their involvement in the gospel-music industry. I knew that besides doing a lot of traveling, all three of them were married and raising children. All those responsibilities intrigued me. I became interested in how they were able to do that, and I learned just how disciplined they are. They didn't make a big deal about it—they just did it.

This is a singing group that in the 1970s was so hurting for money that they almost quit the business. If it hadn't been for their father's unshakable belief that his sons would be successful, you might not have heard of the Williams Brothers today. Now they are not only one of the top singing sensations in the business, but recently published a book that did very well.

I pursued a relationship with the brothers because I enjoyed who they were and their music. I got to find out a lot about them, their children, and their lifestyle. In fact, I wrote all about that in my last book, *Touched by God*. When I signed a record deal in 1990 with Malaco Records, they wrote much of the music for my album. Afterward, I went to Mississippi to visit and spend some time with Leonard and his family.

He and his wife have a very lovely home. They have an older son and a daughter. Both Leonard and his wife are educated and talented, and they both can sing. The couple took me to dinner, and then we drove around Jackson and they showed me points of interest in their community. It was a nice two-day stay. I did a recording with Leonard and his son because he had left the group and formed his own record label. I was trying to help his new record company move along.

At the same time, I became friends with Melvin Williams and Henry Green, who also used to sing with the brothers. Melvin later on fell in love with a woman who worked with me on my show. (I'm good luck for other people as well!)

The Mighty Clouds of Joy

I was about forty years old when I first met Joe Ligon, who is the lead singer of the Mighty Clouds of Joy. This was in 1981, after I came back from performances in Holland and Sweden. My show on BET was attracting bigger and bigger gospel-music stars, and the Mighty Clouds of Joy were one of these groups that stood out among quartet singers.

At that time quartet singing was not a very popular musical craft. People looked down on quartets. They didn't view them as being as aggressive and assertive and knowledgeable as the traditional gospel-music artist. I felt pretty much the same way and paid little attention to quartet singing—I didn't care too much for it.

But the Mighty Clouds of Joy were one of the groups that did stand out among quartet singers, especially their leader, Joe Ligon. He sings as well as anybody can sing in the gospel-music industry.

They came to make an appearance on my show, and about the only conversation I had with them was, "How are you?" "Where do you go from here?"—things like that. It wasn't until some years later that I got to talk to them personally.

I was always very impressed by Joe. He was an undereducated man who was very pleasant and communicated very effectively. Most of the people in the gospel arena are not educated. Most of them stopped their education in high school. They survived by their natural instincts and their ability to sing.

That is why in 1994 I started to sponsor annual retreats. They're almost like a college. They bring gospel-music performers and other people in the industry together to teach them business skills that can help them be even more successful in their careers. I usually hold these retreats in Las Vegas. I do a retreat for record-label producers, one for producers of gospel-music programs, and one for gospel artists.

One of the things I remember telling Joe is that I wanted to do a special on him. I thought he was uniquely gifted in his ability to communicate the gospel sound. He agreed to do it, but then never followed up on my invitation.

Joe surprised me at one of my recent birthday parties. He came and bought me a three-thousand-dollar diamond ring as a gift. I couldn't believe it. I think this was his way of indicating he was sorry that he didn't follow up on the opportunity I had offered him.

I plan to continue to showcase Joe as much as I can on my show. He's about sixty-four years old, and I consider him to be one of the pioneers of gospel music. I want to help him because he's enormously talented and a performer who is a living legend.

My First Grammy Nomination

In 1982 I received my first nomination for a Grammy. It was for the *Come Together* album, and the category was Best Performance by a Black Gospel Duo or Contemporary Gospel Group. It was an amazing moment in my life, and I knew it was only possible because I was recording on a major label like Word Records, and with a great star like Barbara Mandrell.

I remember being at home when my phone rang. And when I heard the news, my first reaction was to thank God. I had never really thought much about the possibility of winning a Grammy, but I always believed that because of the label I was on and the quality work I was producing, that all things were possible.

Of course, if you really want to talk about excitement, it was when I actually won the Grammy in 1984 and Barbara Mandrell was on the project with me. I'll tell you all about that later.

This nomination was just wait-and-see, a hopeful wish, and not much more than that. But it's still wonderful to hear your name mentioned as one of the contenders.

13

Fear and Loathing in South Africa

B obby, how'd you like to go to South Africa?"
  The voice on the other end of the line belonged to Don
Butler, the president of the Gospel Music Association. He called me
one afternoon in 1983 to tell me that there was an opportunity for me
and my organization to travel with him to that country. It was a time
when apartheid was the governing system.

Butler told me that the GMA wanted to approach the South African
church leadership to speak out against apartheid. He said that Christians
from throughout the world would be participating in the retreat that
was going to be held there.

By December 7, when it was time for us to go, I knew that none
of the members from my group would be accompanying me. They
were afraid of going to a country ruled by that system of government.
I hired two people who were once part of my group to go with me,
Charles Miller and Jessie Boyce.

I wanted to be with some people I could depend on in case there
was some trouble. To be truthful, it wasn't an easy decision for me to
make. I was afraid. What would it be like in a country where violence
toward blacks was condoned?

I remember how surprised I was when I landed at the Johannesburg
airport. South Africa was, after all, a black country, and we didn't much

stand out. So we left the airport and headed to our Holiday Inn in downtown Johannesburg.

The next morning some people who worked with Word Records—they were the official host for the trip—picked us up. They took us to this all-white country club for a reception. I walked in the front door with the white people who were part of our group, feeling a little nervous about doing so.

I saw some blacks working there, but they paid me little attention. They knew I had to be an American to get into the door like that. I knew they couldn't go into white men's clubs, and I felt badly about that. It was kind of a guilt trip for all of us, knowing that.

Then we headed for our retreat in Mahalisburg, which was a resort area two hours from Johannesburg. That's where we started the real work of our trip. We heard speeches and songs and listened to talks about how bad apartheid was.

There was one black guy named Caesar who spoke there. I remember that he was powerful-looking and had good knowledge about the situation. He talked about how blacks were treated and what they needed to do to break free of apartheid.

To tell you the truth, as I sat there and listened to his words, I grew increasingly fearful. This kind of talk was forbidden in South Africa during those years. At any moment police could have come in and arrested us.

It was not only the police who could have come in, mistreated, or killed us, but militant black Africans as well. There were a lot of militants who were intent on causing incidents to bring attention to their cause.

One day during the retreat I was talked into going to Soweto. But first we had to go back to Johannesburg. Word Records wanted to do a recording session.

It was kind of unnerving driving back to Johannesburg. We had heard about "Black Friday," and "Black Christmas"—these were days when blacks refused to spend money in that city.

And I had heard talk about what happened to blacks who didn't respect the boycott. They had their hair cut off and were forced to drink oil or other bad substances. It was very cruel. One of those boycotts was now going on, and I didn't want to take the chance of being caught in the middle of something like that.

But Word was our host and they wanted us to make a recording. I couldn't refuse despite all my apprehension. I was scheduled to do a song called "Lord Lift Us up Where We Belong" with a white woman singer from the United States—I think her name was Julie. So there I was in Johannesburg, probably the first black man in Africa to record a song with a white woman.

I'll never forget what a hectic experience that ride to Johannesburg was for me. I was relentless in watching what was going on, because I didn't want to get caught up in something that I could avoid. It was a very dangerous and frightening time in my life.

After we finished recording that night, we headed back to Mahalisburg. It was raining and we decided to take a back road. I remember looking out the window at black people walking along the roads in the rain and the poverty in which they lived. It was very disheartening.

Everywhere I looked I saw very poor black people everywhere. And I understood where they were coming from. It reminded me of my own childhood in Henry, growing up with people who did sharecropping for the white folk. It was the same thing.

I also thought that if my mother knew I was riding along the back roads of South Africa with a white man driving the car while it was raining cats and dogs she would be scared to death for me. I chuckled at that thought and couldn't really blame her.

The next morning we headed out to Soweto. The whole time going there I was again worried about the soldiers. I was really frightened, but I wanted to see how the blacks lived in this notorious township.

We went in with this guy named Matuey-Tuey. He was our guide.

He was a young guy who had just gotten married and was working with the Word staff.

He drove us in, and took us to his modest one-room home. He was very proud of his house. I remember that all they had was a bed, dresser, and a little stove. It really wasn't the best of living conditions.

Then he took us to the library. They had a kind of community center there where they were trying to teach the kids about life and freedom. Caesar, the speaker I had listened to a couple of days before, kind of ran that operation. They needed books. I promised them I would send them some books when I returned to America. Then they showed us a black-owned food store.

We left the food store, which had only the basic essentials. We were driving up a hill when we came across a bunch of kids in the streets. They were eight, nine, ten, eleven years old, and I had heard that they were the backbone of the revolution.

They started heading toward our car. One of them said, "Stop the car, we hear Bobby Jones is in the car." I think at that moment my heart nearly stopped beating! Well, it turned out that my show was being broadcast in South Africa by then, and they had heard of me.

They said, "Oh, Bobby Jones, my brother, we are so glad to see you." I didn't know what to say. I didn't even get out of the car. I just said hello to them and then we continued touring the community.

I got to see Bishop Tutu's house, but he wasn't home at the time. It was a small house and nothing much to be impressed about. I heard that he had another home somewhere that was much grander.

We also drove by Nelson Mandela's home. He wasn't there, either, because he was in prison at the time. Like tourists, we stopped and took pictures of his residence.

Then we saw the more elite areas of Soweto where there were a few nice homes. By then I was ready to get out of there. But first we were taken to one of the senior-citizen hostels, and it was depressing the way these elderly people lived. There weren't even any indoor toilets. It was embarrassing.

I felt very distraught touring this facility. It almost looked like a shack, and old black men were living there. It was pitiful. Even today it's hard for me to describe how I felt about it.

Some time before we arrived, there had been a massacre in Soweto. One bunch of blacks had killed another bunch of blacks because they suspected them of treason.

We were taken to where they housed the survivors of that massacre, and, again, the conditions in which they lived were deplorable. I walked around and talked to these people. They were very cordial to me and I related to them because of their color and their sad condition.

I felt bad seeing them living in such terrible conditions. It was so beneath the standard that we are accustomed to in this country. And they looked so dejected. They were helpless and you could see in their faces that they had no hope.

I didn't know what to say to help them. It was very traumatic for me and the rest of the group. Then we went through areas where there were other refugees being housed. The government was hauling people around in buses and displacing them—putting them in holding areas that reminded me of Nazi concentration camps.

They had hundreds of people stacked up in trucks, and were taking them to different places. There was maybe one water well where everybody had to get their water from. They would fill up buckets, put them on their heads, and take them back to their huts. There were two million blacks living in Soweto under similar substandard conditions. It was awful.

We were on our way to Cape Town to give a couple of performances there.

From my car window I saw natural beauty that is hard to describe—mountains topped with clouds, the ocean, and then Cape Town itself, which is nestled in the hills and surrounded by beautiful mountain peaks.

But despite the beautiful scenery, it was difficult to enjoy the view. Memories were running through my head, of refugee camps and the deplorable living conditions I had seen there.

I had seen sights that shocked me. I had seen places that few Western journalists had been allowed access to. What I got was an insider's view of the horrors of apartheid and what it did to people who were forced to live under such a system. It was a horrifying experience.

When we arrived in Cape Town, what I saw of living conditions for blacks there was as bad as anywhere else. I became very disheartened by what I saw. We stayed in a mansion that was owned by white Christians who were part of the anti-apartheid movement. I remember that the mansion was not very well kept up.

While we were there, we got news that there was a rebellion going on in Johannesburg. It was one of those moments when I was afraid we weren't going to get back home—that we would be caught up in the revolution and maybe be killed.

I remember I became so frightened that I actually cried. I wanted to come home so badly at this point. I actually remember crying out to my mother to help me. I was scared for my life and for the lives of the people I was traveling with.

I could only imagine what was going on at that moment in Johannesburg. Dark images swept my mind, of black people being necklaced, and their cars burned with gasoline; people forced to drink oil, others set on fire. Whites against blacks, blacks against whites, blacks against blacks . . . images so horrible that I literally cried myself to sleep.

I did not want to be necklaced because I was traveling with white people and might be mistakenly viewed by black South Africans as someone who had sold out. I did not want to drink oil or be burned alive. And there was always the fear that at any moment my door would be kicked open and soldiers would throw me in prison or simply kill me on the spot.

Then there is a memory that I will never forget. Here we were in Cape Town, in the midst of the dismal living conditions, giving a gospel

performance. We were surrounded by black faces all longing for freedom. I remember that one of the songs I sang was the Marvin Gaye
hit "What's Going On?"

I'm still haunted by the memory of the sounds of moaning that
came from the audience. It was so piercing I wanted to cry. But I
couldn't cry because we were performing, and I didn't want to appear
as if I was pitying them—although my heart was filled with sadness for
these beautiful and oppressed people.

Sometimes, when I read about people around the world fighting to
be free, I can almost hear those mournful moans from the audience,
and it brings me right back to those days and nights in South Africa.

And then, miraculously enough, we were on an airplane getting ready
to fly home. As I sat on the plane looking out on the runway, there
were many thoughts running through my mind.

Mostly I can recall feeling a heavy sense of sorrow for these people.
I wondered what I could do to help relieve the deplorable conditions
I saw blacks living in wherever I traveled in that country.

I was also thinking about some last-minute sad news that we had
received. Our friend and driver Matuey-Tuey had been necklaced, and
his home burned, for driving us around. Just as I had feared, he was
mistakenly viewed as having sold out. They saw him as part of the
white movement.

I sat there—we all did—filled with sadness for him and his family.
All of us also felt grateful that we had gotten out of South Africa with
our lives. It could just as easily been one of us who suffered such dire
harm.

I vowed that I would never return to that country unless the political situation changed. And, thank the Lord, it finally has. Someday
I might return there, after all.

When I got home some people called what I did "heroic." Maybe so. I never really thought of myself as a hero while I was in that

situation. I hadn't participated much in the civil-rights movement when fighting was taking place on the streets of Nashville or other cities.

Perhaps on an unconscious level this trip to South Africa at the height of apartheid was my way of balancing the score. I had risked my life in another struggle involving black people. So I accepted the compliment. Yes, I was a hero. I did the brave thing and I'm proud of it.

Vice President Al Gore, his wife, Tipper, and me, sharing a warm conversation.

On stage with Albertina Walker (left) and Dorothy Norwood.

Left: Ready to step out for the evening, that's me as a teenager with my cousin Joan and a friend.

Bottom: My mother, Augusta Jones.

The proud graduate.

My brother, James Jones.

Clean-cut and polished in 1970.

Feeling terrific, that's me in 1988.

Vickie Winans (left), Kirk Franklin, Merdeau Gales, and me.

Maya Angelou and me having a great time. This photo was taken
sometime in 1976 or 1977.

Right: That's me posing happily with the native children in Soweto, Africa, in 1983.

Bottom: In Holland with some friends, 1981.

Top: With civil rights activist Rosa Parks.

Left: Chatting with Jerry Lewis during rehearsal for a big show.

Right: Unified in brother-
hood, an organizer and I
give a salute for peace in
Soweto, Africa,
in 1983.

Bottom: The New Life
Singers and me posing
graciously for the
camera.

Vice President Al Gore and Tipper helping me get the crowd to their feet.

Bobby - you've performed a miracle. You make
us look like we can sing!
Love, Tipper

In Las Vegas with Barbara Mandrell in 1989.

With the New Life Singers in 1979.

Left: Conferring
with the
Reverend Jesse
Jackson.

Right: Onstage
proudly accepting
my Stellar Award.

Right: In a spirited performance with Helen Baylor.

Bottom: Linda Carter and me at a gala.

Left: Comedian
Danny Thomas
and me smiling
for the camera.

Right: The
legendary
funnyman
George
Burns and I
share a
laugh.

Right: That's Flip Wilson and me, looking sharp and debonair at an event.

Bottom: Sharing a chuckle with Loretta Lynn.

A young and smiling Bobby Jones, ready to face the
challenges that lie ahead.

14

Gospel-Music Legends and Good Friends

If I could sum up 1982 and 1983 in terms of my career, I'd describe it as a time when I was looking for direction for my television program. I was trying to build an image for the show, and for myself and my New Life group.

I was also working with Barbara Mandrell from time to time, and still teaching at Tennessee State University. I would continue to teach there until 1986, when I lost my interest in teaching at the university level. I'll tell you more about that later.

During the course of these two years I was taping my programs in various television studios, always looking for the best production values. Although I had been thinking of doing some live shows with big audiences, it wasn't very realistic because of the budget involved.

Some of the stations where I taped my program were Channel 8 in Nashville—where the show broadcast for almost eight years—and WKRN-TV, Channel 2, which was a local ABC affiliate also in Nashville.

Until 1989, *Bobby Jones Gospel* was taped in one studio or another; that was the year when, for the first time, we started taping shows in auditoriums outside the studio.

Meanwhile, I kept meeting great gospel singers like Shirley Caesar, Albertina Walker, Yolanda Adams, the Mighty Clouds of Joy, the Williams Brothers—people like that.

Frances Steadman and Marion Williams

Two very special people I met during that period were Frances Stead-man and Marion Williams, who were with a gospel group called the Stars of Faith. Marion was the lead singer and Francis was a quasi lead singer but mostly did background singing for the group.

I never got to know Francis or Marion very well, but I single them out when I think back to those days because they played a special role in gospel music. Marion, for example, was responsible for the "soprano sound." That was her great contribution to the history of gospel music: the way she would sing and perform traditional gospel music with her great soprano voice had never been done before on recordings.

Marion not only could sing traditional gospel music very well, but also had developed these unique body movements to emphasize her message. Watching her onstage was something to see. I just always thought that she was one of the top vocalists.

Francis I knew about through her work with the Clara Ward Sing-ers. She had a rich, deep voice that was quite unusual for a female singer. Her voice was so low, in fact, that I was almost certain she could also sing bass. Even back then I wanted to meet her because I so much appreciated her voice.

Although both these women brought something new to gospel music, the two performers I've always felt the most privileged to meet were Sister Sallie Martin and Willie May Ford Smith. When you talk about the real pioneers of the gospel-music industry, these two artists fit the bill. They were performing in the 1930s when Thomas A. Dorsey, who is considered the father of gospel music, started to write his popularized versions of those traditional songs. Be-fore him, gospel was just a style of music that you could only hear sung in black churches.

If you should ever visit my house, you'll see a plaque hanging on a bedroom wall that was given to me by Sallie Martin in 1987. I must confess that of all the awards that I've received over the years—including the Grammy—this is the one I'm most proud of.

I've always felt connected to gospel music's past, and I've always somehow sensed how important it is to be able to document the works of the older gospel singers.

But it's only of late that I realize how important it was to have had Sallie Martin and Willie May Ford Smith appear on my show. Now, future generations of gospel-music lovers can see and hear two people who were there almost from the beginning.

Sallie Martin

I got to know Sallie Martin through another guy who I knew in the gospel-music business, named Gregory Cooper. He was a musician and had been on my show in the early 1980s with Vanessa Bell Armstrong, who is another powerhouse.

Greg became involved with Sallie's business affairs, and I think they shared an apartment together. He was kind of her adviser or consultant. So it was through my connection with Greg that I got to have many private talks with her.

Sallie shared with me a lot of funny stories that happened with Dr. Dorsey and Willie May Ford Smith and other gospel-music pioneers as they traveled around the country. One of the things she told me was how hard she had to work to get out and promote the music Dr. Dorsey wrote because he was kind of slow and lazy about doing that. So he had to have some women like Sallie and Willie May be the front man for him and do that.

Sallie told me not only was she willing to do so, but she actually loved the responsibility. Of course, she never realized back then that she was helping to build an institution. As is often the case when you're caught up in the middle of a historical moment, all you're really thinking about is that this is a way to make a living, or it's something to do that you believe in. It's a lot easier to see things in hindsight.

Sallie was a wonderful singer in her own right. She had a group called the Sallie Martin Singers. A lot of people got her mixed up with the Roberta Martin Singers. When I got to know her, I found her to be a very unique personality.

She was in her seventies, and was stubborn, aggressive, and determined—a bossy kind of woman. Even in her older age she was still very feisty and trying to perform from time to time. I remember that she was getting a little feeble and required the assistance of a cane.

One day I brought her into the studio, and was fortunate to have Willie May Ford Smith there at the same time. They had been in this movie called *Say Amen, Somebody* and I had them on my show to talk about the movie and the part they had played in the growth of the gospel-music industry.

Of course they proceeded to get into an argument right in front of the cameras. It was funny and kind of wonderful to observe. The argument was about who said what, when, and where to Dr. Dorsey in the Barrett Sisters' apartment in Chicago.

But the way they dealt with it was very funny. And we all laughed about how the two of them would fuss so much. They were the best of friends, but they would not give anything away. Somewhere in my archives I have copies of that show and one day I'm going to pull it out of storage and broadcast it.

Willie May Ford Smith

Willie May Ford Smith, who also was one of the ladies who worked with Dr. Thomas A. Dorsey almost from the beginning, lived in St. Louis. Dr. Dorsey and Sallie Martin lived in Chicago.

Willie May was one of the greatest soloists of that period. Not only could she sing, but she was able to travel and promote Dr. Dorsey's popularized gospel-music songs. She started doing this way back in the 1930s.

I first met her in St. Louis where I used to go and hear her sing. I didn't know Willie May personally back then, but got to know her when I invited her to do my shows in Nashville. She was on my show on several occasions.

Willie was in her seventies, and I remember that she looked motherly. At the time she was not able to totally walk by herself. Like her friend Sallie, she also needed the assistance of a cane. Both these women were in their final days, but they both remained active.

Sister Willie May Ford Smith liked her motherly image. She played that role to the end, and people loved it. It was always "darling this," and "darling that." But when she sang, she was no longer motherly.

Willie May knew she could get attention because of her strong, melodious voice—even in her old age. I think she enjoyed surprising her audience with her youthful, strong voice after portraying this motherly image.

I remember how appreciative she was to me or anyone else that did anything to give her public exposure. She was a real showman. I was impressed when I learned that the University of Missouri had awarded her an honorary doctorate. I thought it was nice of the university to recognize her contribution to the growth of gospel music. She gave me a copy of that program and even autographed it for me. I deeply cherish it.

The Queen of Gospel Music

Thank God for Albertina Walker! This is a woman I have come to know and love over the years. I consider her my closest friend.

It was during one of Reverend James Cleveland's conventions back in the 1970s that I got to meet her. I had been a fan of hers since my freshman days at Tennessee State University, when I first saw her perform with the Caravans. Back then I never had the slightest thought that I'd ever get to meet her.

When I met her, she was just coming out of retirement, thanks to the efforts of Reverend Cleveland who encouraged her to start performing again. Albertina had stopped singing in the sixties when her group, the Caravans, dissolved and members of the group went in their own directions. Shirley Caesar, Dorothy Norwood, and Inez Andrews were some of those other members.

What I remember most about my first meeting with her is that she was very easy to talk to, very likable, and, much to my own surprise, told me that she considered it an honor to meet me.

At the time, I didn't give her as much attention and respect as I should have. I was not really thinking about her back then as one of the pioneers of gospel music, who had been discovered by none other than the great Mahalia Jackson in Chicago.

To me, Albertina was just someone who happened to sing gospel music before I did. There was no overt nostalgia about meeting her because I viewed her as someone on the comeback trail. How wrong could I be?

As time went on, I began to appreciate her more and more—especially when I heard her talk about the places she'd been, the music she performed, and the people she had met over the years.

After meeting her several times, I finally asked her to appear on my show. She loved TV and agreed. That's when I really fell in love with her and our relationship began to grow.

She always expressed a lot of interest in what I was doing, and always wanted me to know some of the things she'd gone through when she traveled with the Caravans during the early years. She sensed my interest in the history of gospel music, and wanted to pass on these stories to me so they wouldn't be forgotten.

Albertina would tell me all about how Shirley Caesar was offstage— such as that great performer's sense of humor. She'd joke about the group being so poor in the early days, that when they were on tour "the only places we could afford to stay were houses where we could see the ground through the floor."

Although the group was poor, Albertina managed to purchase a used Cadillac. She and the girls and the piano player would always travel in

that car. Fortunately for everyone, the Caravans didn't use other instruments at that time, so there was a little more room in the car.

Albertina recalled that they would go and perform somewhere for
a "guarantee" of four or five hundred dollars. "We had no idea that
gospel music would grow like it has and that people would make money
from it," she explained. "We did it because we loved doing it."

One time she talked all about her first album project and how excited she was to go into the studio and record it. On another occasion,
Albertina told me about her visits to Mahalia Jackson's home and how
they would fry chicken together.

Back then, I never knew much about Mahalia Jackson other than
she was a legendary gospel-music star. But from the stories that Albertina told me about her—like the two of them frying chicken—it gave
me a special sense of Mahalia as a person. Those stories about Mahalia
that Albertina related would often keep me laughing.

Albertina is one of my very special people. Whenever I have some
kind of event I try to make sure that she is there. I fly her in, I put her
up in hotels—I would do almost anything for her.

Onstage and offstage she's the same. She's outspoken, lovable, and
likes recognition. She enjoys her title as "Queen of Gospel Music."
And she has a great sense of humor when you get to know her. She's
also a very intelligent lady.

When I first met her, I noticed that she had some kind of respiratory
problem. She couldn't walk long distances. Nowadays she uses a wheelchair a lot. But other than going through this situation, she seems to
be healthy and in good spirits.

One of the things I've always admired about Albertina is her ability
to dress. She loves expensive clothes and jewelry. She's immaculately
dressed at all times, and I'm kind of that same way. She's not only always
well-groomed, but she's a very sophisticated lady.

I was with Albertina just before she got married to her last husband.
I would tease her about marrying this slightly younger man, His name
is Ricco, and she married him eight or nine years ago. Albertina always

took my kidding with good humor and told me that she felt that she needed a companion in her life.

Most of her family has passed away. I think she's down to nephews and cousins because her brother passed not too long ago. One night when we were talking together she cried as she told me how she had buried them all, and how God has kept her and brought her through all of that.

One of the greatest honors she ever could have given me is when she came to my mother's burial. She sang at the funeral. To have Albertina Walker there was a heck of a statement for my community down in Paris. It takes two hours to get to Paris from Nashville, and there are no planes that fly in there.

But that's what she wanted to do. It was her way of letting me know how much she appreciated me. And that's why I always feature her on my show. I always want to make sure that her presence is felt. I think she is deserving of it.

Mahalia Never Could Keep Time

Talking about Albertina reminds me of Mahalia Jackson, who discovered Albertina when she was a young church singer in Chicago. I never met Mahalia, but I recognize her position in the history of gospel music.

I remember that in 1965 she did a special performance at the White House, for Mamie Eisenhower. I recall thinking at the time that she must be a really big star to be black and sing for the president's wife. I was quite impressed.

But when they played her music on the radio, I never liked her singing. And I knew she couldn't keep time. So I never classified her as one of the great gospel-music singers.

I knew that white people loved her, as well as many blacks. But she was never a big draw among her own people. She made her statement in the white world and in Europe.

Shirley Caesar Gets Mad at the Grammy Awards

I remember when I first saw Shirley Caesar perform with the Caravans, how much excitement she brought to the audience. Her dancing, her singing, her quick movements, and her ministering was an exciting thing to watch. She was a little fireball and I liked her a lot.

After the Caravans had gone their separate ways and Shirley became an independent act, it was interesting to watch her develop. Not many of the singers who left the group were able to have a solo career as profound as Shirley's. Dorothy Norwood was one of the girls who did do well on her own.

I finally was able to get Shirley to do my *Bobby Jones Gospel* show in about 1983. I met her through a friend of mine by the name of Al Hobbs. He used to date her and tell me about Shirley. And watching her on my show—boy, was she energetic! When she goes for it, she really goes for it!

Since then, she's done my show many times and we developed a relationship that went beyond talk about the gospel-music business. When we were together we'd talk about our boyfriends and girlfriends. We're about the same age, although I always thought she was older than me because she carried herself in a much more serious manner.

Sometimes we'd tease each other, and I'd say something and make out like I was trying to hit on her. And she'd respond as women do. But I really didn't have a crush on her—it was just good-natured teasing. I even remember once chasing Shirley down a hotel hallway, but she wouldn't let me catch her. We had fun together like that. And we'd share a lot of things together and also talk about the road, different record labels, and concert attendance.

I remember one time I was taping my show on Channel 2 and she had been invited to appear. I knew that she had just lost her mother a few days before, so I didn't think she'd make it. She was very close to her mother and was grieving over the loss. So I said to myself, *She's not coming.*

But to my surprise she showed up and gave a performance. As I was doing an interview with her after her songs she began to weep a little bit.

"Can you do this?" I asked.

"I can do it, I'm a professional," she replied.

That's how Shirley is. She's a trouper. Today she continues to appear before heads of state and she's always appearing on major television programs. She's also stepped up her efforts as a minister.

I remember visiting her church one day when I went to Raleigh, North Carolina, which is where she's from. I had the opportunity to say hello to her church members, and I said some encouraging things to Shirley in terms of helping her to build her church.

Another time I was with Shirley was in Los Angeles when we went there for the Grammy Awards. She had been nominated for one of the categories and didn't win. I can still recall how disturbed she was. She felt that her music was quite accomplished and that she should have won the Grammy.

So I had to remind her that this was an awards show, and that the votes had little to do with how good you really were. But she wouldn't buy that. She wasn't feeling good about not winning.

What that indicated to me about her was that Shirley is a serious contender. She wants to be recognized for the work she does. She believes that whatever she does, is done very well. She wants that level of respect.

While I think that's great, her reaction to not winning the Grammy Award still kind of surprised me. I thought she'd be a bit more modest about the work she does for the Lord. But she wasn't at all—and she let you know it!

After that, from time to time we'd meet on the road. I was invited to her wedding, but I didn't go. I did wonder why she was marrying an older man, but when I saw them together they seemed compatible, and I'm very happy for her.

But whenever we speak, we still joke and tease each other. She was the one who always pushed me to get married. Nowadays Shirley seems a bit more relaxed. But she is still serious about her music. Most of all, Shirley Caesar is a lot of fun. She likes to laugh, she likes to eat, and she likes to joke with people. Shirley's a very down-to-earth individual.

But there are times when she's in front of certain types of people that she doesn't let her fun side be seen. That's when she's maintaining her image as a pastor or as a Holy Ghost–filled gospel singer. She's very protective of herself, and I don't think that's bad. Whatever setting she's in, Shirley wants to make sure that she's recognized and that her ministry is effective to the point where people respond to her.

She deserves that respect. I've seen her ministry in action and it's impressive to observe. I've seen her suddenly stop singing and start preaching and even lay hands on people for healing to help them overcome adversity and other problems.

I consider Shirley one of the first ladies of gospel music because of her performance ability and how she interacts with her audiences in delivering her message. In fact, she is currently known as the First Lady of Gospel Music. They call her that because she was the first lady on her record label to sing gospel music. I can think of many other reasons for her to have that very fitting title.

Looking Ugly on a Country-Music Special

I grew up listening to country music, because it was the only music we had on the radio back in Henry and Paris, Tennessee. Even today I'm familiar with many of the country-music stars and the Nashville sound. Although I'm not in love with country music, there are some songs that I do like.

Because of my association with Barbara Mandrell, who is part of the country-music industry, other country-music artists began to ask us to come and tour with them. These country artists were also asking me if they could do my show. So for a while I had country stars like Ricky Skaggs, Dolly Parton, and Loretta Lynn appearing on my gospel-music program.

One star who asked us to tour with him was Ronnie Milsap, who is blind. I agreed and we toured with Ronnie for a while in 1983, singing mostly contemporary Christian music. Ronnie was one of the most profound and talented entertainers I've ever worked with, and I was proud to be part of his entourage. I found him also to be very inspiring because of how he handled himself despite his handicap.

We traveled and performed at several major events together. I remember being so impressed with his performances, that each night I eagerly waited for the opportunity to watch his presentation. I was learning stage techniques from him.

The highlight of my association with Ronnie was that I was able to do an excellent TV special with him—except for one problem that had to do with the way I looked.

Although I was excited about doing the TV special with him, things did not go as smoothly as I had hoped. Just before the special, I had developed this growth on my forehead. And I didn't want to go on TV looking like that.

It was a very traumatic moment for me because, as you know by now, I'm very sensitive to my appearance. But this knot on my forehead kept getting bigger and bigger. So I thought that maybe I should have it removed before I did the show.

So off I go to my doctor, and he tells me it will be a simple, in-office procedure. What happened was that he was correct as far as it being a simple procedure. But when I returned home, instead of relaxing I started working and moving around and doing things.

The blood drained down to under my eyes. Now my eyes looked blackened and I looked absolutely horrible. But I still remained excited about appearing on the special, and decided that I was going to do it no matter how bad my appearance.

The next day—the day we were going to tape the show—I didn't look any better and that disturbed me. But I did it anyway. We did one of our tunes, and I remember that Ray Charles was one of the guest performers. And Ronnie was good, as usual.

But when I think back to my appearance, I still feel a bit embarrassed. Millions of people who had never seen me before were watching the special, and I can't help but wonder what they must of thought about this singer who looked like he had just come out of some barroom brawl.

15

Some Sour Grapes Over
My Grammy Award

What can I say about winning a Grammy Award with Barbara Mandrell? I remember how excited I was about going to the awards ceremony. I knew that we had been nominated, but I thought it would be nearly impossible for us to win.

I'd been through this before in 1982, when I was nominated for my *Soul Set Free* album and nothing happened. Now, two years later, I pretty much expected the same result. This time, however, I was nominated in the category of Best Vocal Duo for a Soul Gospel Performance. The song that was up for an award was a duet with Barbara from our *Come Together* album. It was entitled "I'm So Glad I'm Standing Here Today." And by the end of the evening I certainly was!

I learned that Word Records wasn't sending anybody along to support me, and that I would be attending the awards ceremony by myself. Even though I had been nominated for an award, my Christian record company still wasn't thrilled about a black man and a white woman performing a Las Vegas act together.

Even Barbara wouldn't be there for support, because she was performing at some benefit. She had told me that if we won the Grammy, she considered it my award because of all the work I had done on that album.

Since I had two tickets to the event, I called a Nashville friend, Alfonso Hughes, and asked him to come along. So we headed out to Los Angeles together.

On that airplane ride, my only thoughts about the upcoming awards ceremony was what I should wear. I ended up renting a tuxedo and wondering where I would be sitting and who would be sitting next to me. Boy, I had some great fantasies during that plane ride!

It turned out that our seats were in the back of the auditorium. But I was still excited. All the big names were there—gospel stars like the Winans and the Clark Sisters. I figured the Winans would get it because they were so popular.

They went through all the awards and finally got to the gospel category. All the stars around me started to fidget nervously. When they called my name I think I became kind of mummified. I was so shocked, that I can't even remember walking to the stage.

The next thing I remember is being up there and feeling very nervous. I didn't have any acceptance speech ready and I don't even remember what I said. I think I thanked Barbara Mandrell, the record label, and the New Life Singers. I don't even remember if I thanked God—but I hope I did.

When I left the stage I felt that this was one of the proudest moments in my professional career. But there were some gospel stars who disagreed with my win. I had gotten that feeling even before I won the Grammy.

There was a break between the early awards and the major awards. So you would go to the lobby area and hang out. It was there that I encountered some gospel artists who weren't very kind to me, hinting that the "I'm So Glad" song should not have been nominated because it was written by Joe Cocker. In fact, I later learned that some people in the industry had met with the Grammy board and told them they didn't feel that Barbara and I should have been nominated for a gospel-music award.

I didn't know that all this was going on behind the scenes. And I didn't know that even months afterward there was an effort to have my award rejected. They kept objecting that the song wasn't really a gospel song.

That year the Grammy Awards' gospel category wasn't televised, so the first person I called was my mother to tell her I had won. She was so excited and she congratulated me. Then I called members of my group and I called Barbara. She was just as excited as I was—this was her first and only Grammy. After that, everywhere we'd travel to perform, she'd mention to the audience that this was her first and only Grammy, and that she won it with Bobby Jones.

After the Grammy presentations were over, I went to some of the celebrations and then returned home to Nashville. The story of my winning the Grammy was in *Jet* magazine, and all the local papers covered it.

But despite all the accolades, winning the Grammy didn't do much to jump-start my career at the time. I had expectations that it would, but with no personal management, and a record company that was not solidly behind me, nothing happened. Also, maybe it was because the album had a lot of country music on it.

The Jealous Winans

During the Grammy Awards I met the Winans for the first time. We were both staying at the Biltmore Hotel in downtown Los Angeles. I had heard their music and I thought that the whole family were good singers. I also made the mistake of assuming that gospel-music people just loved each other because we were all church folk. I didn't know the serious kind of separatism and jealousies that existed in reality.

When I met them they were seated in a restaurant. I got a chance to meet CeCe and BeBe's mother and father, who were very nice. I knew that the Winans had been nominated in the same category that Barbara and I had been nominated for. I didn't think it mattered all that much to them that they had not won the award. But it did. And they treated me like I was nothing.

In fact, I later learned that the Winans family was part of the group that was lobbying against Barbara and myself having won the Grammy Award. Marvin Winans put out the word that the song wasn't gospel and that the only reason I had been nominated was because of Barbara Mandrell.

I thought differently. I considered myself a gospel singer even though I was doing contemporary Christian versions of gospel music. Looking back, I suspect that maybe a lot of black people in Nashville hated me because I was singing with Barbara and other white stars like Ronnie Milsap.

I guess what they didn't understand was all I was trying to do was make a career for myself—and white people had the money and the access to the world of show business. That's the reason why I did that. I knew that eventually I would be able to do what I wanted to do—which is sing traditional gospel music.

I also remember that when I first met BeBe and CeCe at one of evangelist Jim Bakker's televised shows, they were not very friendly toward me. It didn't seem to matter at all to them that I had sung with Barbara Mandrell and had my own popular television show. Today, however, we are good friends.

I've had BeBe and CeCe on my show, as well as their parents. And I have never lost respect for them. Despite the treatment I once suffered from the Winans, I have always respected them. I thought they were good singers, and I still do to this day.

At that time, however, I was just a little floored by their negative personalities.

The Dove Award

A month after winning a Grammy, Barbara and I won the Dove Award, which is the most prestigious award in the Christian music industry. Winning this award didn't have the same effect on me as winning the Grammy. My reactions were much more contained. I certainly accepted it with much delight—it was my first and only Dove—and I hoped it would add to my growth as a performer. But it's hard for me to personally assess whether it did or didn't.

Between the Grammy, the Dove, an NAACP Achievement Award for "Outstanding Community Service" with Project Help, and my accomplishments on television, 1984 was a pretty special year for me. All these awards were high points of that year.

Aside from such honors, much of that year was spent doing concerts, teaching at the university, traveling, meeting new artists like the Fifth Dimension, and Ben Moore from the Spinners, and generally enjoying life.

A Friend Goes Blind

When I first heard about a singer named Reverend James Moore, it was back in the seventies. James was living in Memphis at the time, and he called me and left a message that he would like to do my show. I had one of his albums and was not impressed by him at the time, so I remember that I didn't even bother to return his phone call. Little did I know that years later I would consider this remarkable talent one of my best friends.

The first time I met James was in the 1980s in Detroit, at one of the Gospel Music Workshops of America. I was very impressed by his performance, but distressed by his appearance. He was overweight, and had only two or three front teeth. I thought, *Why can't a guy who can sing like this fix himself up?*

But I will admit that once James opened up his mouth to sing, people tended to forget what he looked like. He is an incredible performer. His voice is strong and very steady. The more I saw him, the better I got to like him.

I also noticed that he had taken a liking to me. He liked what I was doing with my show and wanted to be on it. And because I now realized just how talented he was, I let him perform several times. I kept bringing him on TV and people who watched our show really started responding to him and buying his music because of the exposure he was getting. And James loved it.

I remember during one taping, I had him deliver the principal address to the young people in our viewing audience. James did an excellent job of that, which made me realize he was a natural-born preacher. And that led me to listen more intensely not only to his music, but to the lyrics to his songs as well. Our friendship continued to grow to the point where, today, I consider him one of my best friends.

Then in the 1990s James suddenly lost his eyesight from diabetes and kidney disease. We spoke a lot on the phone, and I gave him as much encouragement as I could. By this time I had become like a big brother to him.

I remember when James first called me that he sounded scared.

"What's going on?" I said.

"I was sitting in the hospital watching TV, and all of a sudden I didn't see it," James said. "I rubbed my eyes, and was able to watch TV again, and then I couldn't see at all."

My heart sank as I listened to his words.

"You're going to come through this and you're going to get better," I told him. Then we talked about faith and I told him that he must continue to believe that the Lord would restore his eyesight.

It was a frightening moment both for James and myself. But over all these years he has continued to keep his faith that the Lord will someday heal him, and that his loss of eyesight is only temporary.

This isn't the first setback that James has suffered. As a teenager, he lost three of his younger siblings in a tragic house fire. Later, just when his career was beginning to take off, James lost his dearest friend and manager. With all this tragedy in his life, you'd think that James would react by walking around in a constant state of depression.

But not this gospel-music star. Even today, despite all his physical disabilities and the fact that he is often confined to a wheelchair, James continues to push forward and do things that many people who are in good health won't do. That's what makes him so special to me—his desire to continue to sing and praise the Lord even while he grapples with illness.

James may not have his eyesight, but he sees the Lord as well as any soldier in the gospel army. I'm very impressed with him and his boldness.

Back to the Holy Land

I returned to Israel in 1994. The Israeli government wanted to make a film to help promote tourism, so they contacted the Gospel Music Association, who contacted me.

I was happy to be going back to the land of Jesus and His disciples. By now I was familiar with that country, but this time we were getting a higher class of treatment because we were going to do some work for the government.

Only a few members of my singing group went on this trip. They didn't want to commit because the Israeli government wasn't paying us for our time. But I've always looked at things as opportunities, and so I was anxious to go. Something might happen on that trip to elevate my career.

It was a great trip, although it was unbearably hot. We visited twenty-two Christian sites to make the film for the Department of Tourism. Here we were in the middle of an Israeli summer with scorching temperatures and we're running around the desert in this van carrying movie lights.

I was happy with the exposure I got from participating in that promotion. It was shown in ninety-nine countries, and people all around the world got to see me. At the end of the filming we did a concert at the Jerusalem Theatre, which was sold out. We were the only act, and we did it with just a couple of our girl singers and one of our ex-members, Oliver Sueing. But the audience loved us and they were dancing in the aisles.

16

Forgiving My Father

My father started to become ill around 1985. He was living in Paris, Tennessee, with my mother, and was having problems with his circulation.

I'd seen him over the years on regular home visits, but now that he was ill I was beginning to feel better about being in his presence and sharing things with him about my life because he wasn't as intoxicated as he usually was.

He was the one who really opened the door for that better relationship between us. He had become proud of me and the work I was doing—and he was even able to express to me and his friends how proud he was. Little by little we became more positive toward each other.

My father was also treating my mother differently toward the end—and even going to church! I was elated about all that, so things were starting to come together with our relationship.

But I don't think I talked much about my childhood days with him. I guess I felt the more we left that subject alone, the better off we would be. But I did let him know I was proud of his new behavior, and that he was not like he used to be. And in his own kind of way he apologized to me for some of the things he'd said and done, and that he had not given me any support—financial or otherwise—during my college years. He told me he just hadn't known how to share those positive things with me, but that he really did care and was very proud of me when I went to college. And there was one day that I embraced him!

I guess I just wanted our relationship to happen—a relationship that I never had as a kid. All my life I've regretted that I never had a father who was a positive role model. I so much wanted that solid family structure. And now that my mother was no longer in harm's way, and my father was being kind to me, that made it possible for me to embrace him. It was a time of healing. I guess by that gesture I was trying to form the family that been interrupted by my father's drinking.

Thinking back, I remember that as a youngster it was difficult for us to even have a Thanksgiving or Christmas dinner together. Either one or both of my parents would be drinking and disrupt the flavor of Christ's birthday. It's hard to celebrate a spiritual moment when somebody is drunk.

All through my childhood I thought that the reason why my parents never embraced me the way I wanted to be embraced was because I had been naughty. Their love seemed to be passed on to my brother and my sister instead of me. Even when my brother was not living at home, I could tell how much my parents respected him when they would mention his name. I had never felt that kind of respect, and I thought that maybe I had brought it upon myself. I thought that maybe it was my actions and my aggressiveness that didn't allow them to reach out to me as much as they did to my brother and sister. So I had become a loner and learned to fend for myself.

Even my cousins often treated me the way my parents did. They were kind to my sister and gave her things right in front of me. And they wouldn't give me anything. But I remember that sometimes they did include me, and those were good moments in my life—to be included.

I guess a lot of that kind of treatment had to do with me being more education-oriented than regular country like all the other kids in that small town were. So as a result I experienced a lot of rejection and neglect.

One of the reasons why I loved my grandmother so much is that she always showed me a lot of love and never neglected me in my early years. And when she passed away I lost a lot of that, because neither my mother or father gave me that kind of support. It's also the reason why I live very well now. I have a beautiful house and my house is filled with beautiful things. All my life I worked extra hard to succeed because I wanted to show my parents that I *was* somebody.

The funny thing is, that despite all that kind of treatment—especially from my dad—I think I always loved him anyway. And it was in that simple embrace so many years later, that I was able to express the love that had been buried in me for so long.

My father eventually became sicker. He had to go to the hospital in Nashville where they removed one of his legs because of the seriousness of the circulation problem. That was sad for us, and we thought it would be fatal for him.

But he came through the surgery and was able to move around slowly. Not long afterward, however, his other leg had to be removed as well. Then he started staying at a nursing facility in Paris because my mother could not handle him at home. She was getting older and couldn't do many of the things that he needed.

Now everything was starting to go wrong with him. He was struggling with emphysema, and couldn't breathe. Then he had a stroke. He couldn't talk for two years. He could understand us, but he couldn't respond.

My father really suffered toward the end. I remember spending a Wednesday and Thursday with him at the nursing home, and that Friday morning he passed away. He had slipped into a coma. I remember that my mother and sister and I all breathed a sigh of relief that he didn't have to suffer anymore.

His death was a sad moment in my life. No matter what, he was still part of me. I had grown to love him, and I was very shaken by his death. I grieved a lot after he passed. I think, of everyone in my family, I grieved the hardest and the longest. My sister was quiet and so was my brother at the funeral, but I was very emotional.

Even today I still miss him. I think about him often. I remember a lot of things about him. There are many times when I try to ponder where things I do come from, and I wonder if it comes from my mother or my father. I also think about the days when I was much younger, and the things my parents had to do to survive while they were trying to raise us. And I sometimes wonder where all the energy I have came from.

I assume that all my intellectual qualities come from my mother; I just assume that because she ran things and she was the literate one. My father was illiterate.

But I'm still perplexed about what characteristics I inherited from my father. Did I get all my energy and love of hard work from him? I guess the characteristics I pick out the most are those that had nothing to do with his drinking. When he wasn't under the influence of alcohol, he was a lovable person and he wanted to be accepted.

He had a shy attitude, and I have that, too. I think that's where it came from. When I think about him in his final days, it's a total reversal of how I thought about him earlier in life when he wreaked so much havoc in our lives because of his inability to discipline himself. Those were very bad years for me.

And if I've never involved myself with alcohol or smoking in a major way, I guess that's also a result of my father's behavior. I just never wanted to become addicted to anything the way he was.

I'm sometimes asked why I talk about my father's alcoholism in public the way I'm doing in this book. The answer is that I want other people who have experienced a similar kind of abuse to know that they can survive in such a household just as I did.

I don't do it to ridicule him. I'm just trying to say that you can overcome these things, too.

Feeling Rejected

Thinking about my father and those childhood days also makes me think about my relationships with my brother and sister. My brother was always distant from me and he never played the important role of big brother to me. I feel that when I was trying to make it through college and different things in my life, he should have been more supportive toward what I was doing. He really never was. He left home and, like my parents did, left me to fend for myself. And I did! My brother and I are closer now than we've ever been, but I still carry those memories with me.

My sister was lovable and was there for me, but she was so quiet that she hardly ever talked. She seldom commented on anything. She would just laugh or smile—she's still that way. She would always say that my mother and I talked enough for her. I also remember being just as jealous of my sister as I was of my brother because of the way my parents treated her. It was always with more respect and love than they treated me.

Another thing I think about is that maybe I was treated so badly because my parents really didn't want another child in their lives. It's confusing because as I grew older, my mother and I became like one person. We became so special to each other, that I really don't know what happened in those early years to make her treat me the way she did—why she and my father had so rejected me.

I remember times when I was doing a concert and my mother would be there in the audience. Afterward we would have a chance to talk. I would sometimes raise this question. She would get upset with me for doing so. She wouldn't want to talk about it. To this day I'll never know if she knew the impression her behavior had made on my life and how it affected me.

These feelings of rejection that I experienced also kept me from getting married for many years—I didn't marry until I turned fifty-nine. It's not that I didn't have plenty of opportunity or plenty of relationships; I was afraid of the commitment because, I think, I was afraid of eventually being hurt or rejected like I once had been by my parents. I've never had a very positive image of family life because mine was so disruptive. I felt safer being on my own and doing things my own way, like I've done since I was a child. So I stayed away from marriage for many years. I opted for privacy rather than a relationship.

Believe it or not, rejection is something I still struggle with today, despite all my success. I've always thought that what I accomplished by bringing gospel music to television was kind of miraculous and Divinely guided. After all, I had no financial support. The only support I had was from the Lord.

But despite such success, deep down I would have loved some real appreciation for my efforts—at least from my family. But it wasn't until my later years that my mother, my father, my sister, and my brother finally understood what was going on with me, and those fears of rejection that I still harbored.

Until only quite recently, even my cousins didn't know about me and my professional struggles. My brother's kids also knew very little about me, and that made me feel rejected. If it were me and I had kids, I would have demanded that they watch what their uncle was doing on television. I've always wanted to be a role model for my nieces and nephews, but they never got into me. Just the other weekend one of my nieces called me and said, "Uncle Bob, you know I'm just finding out who you are. I am so proud to be your niece, Uncle Bob."

That was such a joy for me to hear. I had always wanted to hear that but I would never say anything about it to my brother and sister. So getting that phone call really filled me with a lot of joy.

I don't know why it's been like this—these struggles to not feel rejected. I'm always trying to get things done because I know who I am—I've always had a good heart; but people never seem to know who I really am and what's in my heart.

The Reverend Milton Brunson

I met the late Reverend Brunson in the early 1970s when he was leading a community choir that had no real status; it was just a church activity. But even back then I was impressed by his choir and church activities. In the 1980s he resurfaced on the national level with a choir that gained him all kinds of attention.

He was an arrogant man, difficult to get to know. So I didn't spend a lot of time with him. I knew where my boundaries were in terms of getting into his company; but once I gained some notoriety with my TV show, he introduced himself to me again.

Despite his personality, to me he was a kind of role model in the gospel-music industry. I really admired the contributions that he had made over the years to gospel music. I still felt that his singers thought too much of themselves. But they were big-city people from Chicago, and sometimes city folk have a different attitude in the way they carry themselves.

It was amusing that when he finally remembered me from earlier years, what he recalled most about me was that I was always so fastidious and wanted everything to be in place. I guess that was true. It still is.

But Reverend Brunson never really got to know me on a deep level. I knew more about him than he knew about me. He had only observed me from my television show, which he said he watched every week. We stayed friends until he passed away, but we never had any real personal interaction. I just wanted to mention him in this book because he is part of gospel-music history.

There's Nobody Better Than Vanessa Bell Armstrong

It was back in the 1970s that I was first introduced to Vanessa. I had my *Nashville Gospel Music Show* going at the time. Gentry McCrary,

Vanessa's producer, came to my home on Eleventh Avenue North. He had a demo that Vanessa had recorded, and asked my opinion about it.

I listened to it and her voice was nice but the songs went nowhere. I told this to him; I gave him my honest opinion. Well, he listened to me and went and changed the whole album. He added more material and that album went on to become a hit.

There was one song on that album that was very popular. It was called "Peace Be Still." It had already been a hit for Reverend James Cleveland, and she kind of redid it. It was that song, which Vanessa did on the Onyx label, that turned her into a household name.

Some time after that, Gentry brought Vanessa in to tape my show and I had a chance to meet her personally. I remember that my first impression of her was that she was short. But I was blown away by her ability to sing the way she did. Vanessa had this "young Aretha Franklin" sound, and I would have loved to have had her in my backup group. But by then she was an accomplished soloist. She did, however, end up singing with me on one of my latest albums—*Just Churchin'*.

As the years went by, we became good personal friends. I had hosted several of her new album presentations, and she did several specials with me. We would come together in concert performances and we did several industry-related events together. So we had a lot of time to get to know each other. I considered her a premier gospel artist, and I still feel that way. There's nobody better than Vanessa.

I got to know her family, her daughters, her mother, and her father, who is a minister. I even visited his church. Vanessa is a single parent, although most of her children are now grown.

I remember that she had some difficulties raising her kids after her divorce. Part of the problem was the time commitment because she was quickly becoming a superstar. And although I wouldn't go as far as saying that I was influential in her life, I like to think that the talks I had with her about her situation helped to keep her family in the proper order. It all worked out. Today Vanessa has a terrific relationship with all her kids. I had a chance to notice that at one of her recording sessions. They all came to support her.

One of Vanessa's sisters is a recording artist as well, and another sister manages her business—her name is Margaret Bell. Margaret also has enormous singing ability, but she married a professional football player and it kind of distracted her from the recording business. She didn't need the money after she married this professional athlete.

So the whole family is one positive unit. I like that, and I'm always appreciative when I see how they interact with each other. Sometimes when I observe them together, a moment of sadness sweeps my heart and I wish my family had been this way when I was a child.

If you wonder what Vanessa is like offstage, let me tell you. She is shy, and sometimes it's difficult for people to understand that. Once you can get through that shyness, you find a sweet and talented and friendly woman—one I am proud to know and have worked with. And she keeps a positive attitude despite the difficult times she went through with her divorce. Vanessa once told me that it would have been quite easy for her to feel sorry for herself, but, "I dealt with the issue rather than try to escape it."

If you want to get an even more intimate glimpse of Vanessa's pain, then listen to her music. In songs like "Tears" she often alludes to the emotional pain she once suffered and how she managed to get through that difficult time with God's help.

Vanessa once told me something that has stuck with me and is good advice for everyone. She said, "If you're feeling hurt, discouraged, or rejected, and you can't cry anymore, then turn to prayer."

I'm proud of Vanessa. I look forward to watching her grow tremendously in the gospel-music industry. She is constantly growing in her personal life, always extending a helping hand to others.

There isn't a year that goes by that I don't learn something new about Vanessa's generosity. She's always lending a helping hand, whether it's financially, physically, or spiritually. She's a faith-driven performer on a mission from God.

Two Costume Changes in a Funeral Casket

It was a personal friend of mine who first introduced me to the Reverend James Cleveland back in the early 1970s. Reverend Cleveland had come to Nashville and offered one of the guys who used to sing with me—Alfonso Hughes—a job as his road manager. But even before Alfonso introduced me to the King of Gospel Music, I used to follow Reverend Cleveland around and listen to his music whenever I could. I was always a great fan of his.

In the 1980s, when my gospel TV program was nationally syndicated on the BET network, I wanted James to appear on my show. But he didn't want to do it unless I paid him. The show wasn't set up to have a stipend for guests. Guests would appear free of charge for the national exposure the program offered them. So Reverend Cleveland declined my offer.

I think he looked at my TV show as being in competition with him and his Gospel Music Workshops of America. I think he felt I was challenging his stature as the King of Gospel Music. I just sensed from his words and his actions that he was somewhat envious of me.

When James passed away in the late 1980s from some kind of viral infection I attended his funeral. I was actually surprised at the attention everyone gave me. I hosted his home-coming service before the funeral, and there was such politeness toward me from his family and staff. I thought this was all a bit ironic because of the rivalry that had been established between the two of us. But nonetheless, here I was hosting his funeral service.

As I waited for the service to begin, my thoughts drifted back to the last time I had seen him. It was at an appreciation program they had held for him in Los Angeles at the Dorothy Chandler Pavilion. After that program, I had gone to his home, and Reverend Cleveland kidded me that I had twice performed at his church and he hadn't had to pay me. We both shared a good laugh at that.

Reverend Cleveland's funeral was held at the Shriners' Auditorium in Los Angeles. That site was selected because few other auditoriums in the city were big enough to hold all the people who came to witness his home-going.

I remember being astounded at sharing the stage with so many other gospel celebrities—people like Shirley Caesar, Albertina Walker, and Al Hobbs, who is president of the Religious Announcers Guild and a board member of the Gospel Music Workshops of America.

Everyone in that auditorium recognized that this was a special moment in the history of gospel music. It was the passing of the King of Gospel Music. Sitting there, I couldn't help but reflect about the many years I had seen James Cleveland perform his onstage magic.

I also reflected on the great gospel-music organization that he had created—the Gospel Music Workshops of America—and his contributions to gospel music in general.

There was an amusing moment during that service. Reverend Cleveland had an open casket, and twice they dressed him in different outfits. I don't think I'd ever seen anybody laid out like that before—with costume changes!

I was also a little embarrassed by the situation because I noticed the bottom of his shoes were scuffed. I thought that if they were going to go through all the trouble of changing his costume, they could have put some new shoes on him. Overall, I don't think I really appreciated the way he was laid out. I would have preferred a more conservative viewing.

I remember looking around that great auditorium and seeing so many people there, it amazed me. I was also a bit startled when they buried Reverend Cleveland in a vault. That was the first time I had seen something like that. At all the burials I had attended in my life, people were lowered into the ground. But I knew that because of his prestige and money, they were able to put him away in this manner—and they did!

After his death, I was disappointed to learn that Reverend Cleveland had given little thought to the future of his GMWA business. He had failed to appoint people to certain jobs to make certain that this valuable organization functioned smoothly.

Not only was his convention business in disarray, but also his church and his personal affairs. I thought that a man with that kind of intelligence, and having been sick as long as he was, would have considered the possibility of his passing and made provisions for people to handle his estate.

He didn't, and there were all these terrible newspaper articles about his personal and business holdings. People were trying to sue his estate. Even his daughter had no idea about his financial arrangements. Only one other person had worked with him trying to manage all his business, and that person's business practices were very questionable.

My Teaching Days Are Over

I had completed my doctorate at Vanderbilt University in 1980, and eventually returned from my leave of absence at Tennessee State University to resume my teaching duties.

A busy six years followed, and I found myself more and more distracted by all the television work I was doing. I also started to lose my interest in teaching. The program I was teaching in had been restructured, and I found myself with less freedom and time to tend to all the things I was doing outside the classroom. The university was requiring that I spend more hours there than the typical college professor.

I became convinced that I couldn't teach and work on my television career at the same time, and do both jobs effectively. That bothered me because I'm a perfectionist. I had to quit one or the other. It wasn't an easy decision to make.

On the one hand, I had established my rank and tenure at the university, and that hadn't been easy to acquire. There was a lot of security for me teaching college. I was guaranteed a job for a long time. On the other hand, I was making more money with the gospel shows and was also able to travel. So I prayed over it and also tried to get some idea from the Black Entertainment Network about my future there.

I told Bob Johnson that I was thinking of resigning my job at the university and going full-time with the station; I asked him if he thought I would be around for a while, so that I wouldn't be jobless. He indicated to me that the station planned to keep me.

I also consulted with my mother, different instructors at the university who were friends of mine, and Dr. Ruby Martin, who was the head of my department. I talked the situation over with some personal friends of mine as well. Everybody was kind of saying at this point that I should give television a chance.

My mother cautioned me to check my options carefully, and to make sure that the television job would take care of me financially. When I told her how much I was making with my entertainment career as opposed to my salary at the university, it didn't take much to convince her that the gospel ministry was my future. I loved her for being there for me and supporting me.

Ultimately it was God's decision, and I believe He guided me to resign my university post. I also knew in my heart that television is what I really wanted to do. This was a real turning point for me, because for the first time I was leaving academia for good and making the entertainment industry my full-time career.

I remember that when I went back to get my belongings, already having written a letter of resignation, I felt a certain emptiness, sadness, and uncertainty; I was even wondering if they would let me come back if I needed to. I had spent fifteen enjoyable years with the university. I was a great teacher, and I had brought a lot of my experience to my students that I don't think they would have gotten from any other instructor in my department at that time.

They had benefited from the things I'd done in my life, the places I'd been, the things I'd seen, and the experiences I'd had. I knew that over the years, I had given all my students a solid background in communication skills.

On the other hand, I felt elation and a sense of freedom. No longer would I have to report every morning at a certain time to the university or go to lunch at a certain time. My lifestyle was such that I didn't like these kinds of restrictions put on me.

Now I was free to devote more time to my TV production. I'd be better able to concentrate on getting more well-known artists to appear, and to plan for the future—and I had great plans. I wanted to bring gospel music to a position of respectability through a good format, great singers, guests who articulate the cultural importance of gospel music, and by serving as a role model.

What I wanted to do most of all is make certain that this music of my people would never die. That it would continue to live on through the medium of television.

Another Flop

Now that I could concentrate on my creative activities, in addition to my duties with two television programs I recorded an album for Light/ Lexicon Records. It was called *Another Time*. There was a new group of New Life singers backing me up by now, and I was very excited about doing this album. I had already done the two albums for Word Records—*Soul Set Free* and *Come Together*.

I had decided to switch to this label because it was the same company that had made Andrae Crouch so popular—and I was such an admirer of his.

I remember how pleased the president of the company was about having us. It appeared that this was going to be a wonderful relationship. However, the album ended up being another flop. The same day my album was released, the company went out of business, so most of the albums were never sent out to radio stations. That made it a terrible situation for me.

I had the masters, and copies of the record, so I managed to get some records out. I was able to distribute the album to my fans through my TV show—that was the good side of it.

Another positive thing that came out of this disaster was meeting a young woman who was doing work for the record company at the time, by the name of Vickie Mack Lataillade. Vickie was the one who had let me know what had happened to my album. Never in my wildest dreams did I ever imagine that one day I would be recording on a record label which she owned—GospoCentric, which also produces Kirk Franklin.

People sometimes ask me how I came up with the *Another Time* name for my album. The answer is cunningly simple. I wanted to have an album that started with the letter *A*. I realized that on various voting ballots for best records, that they always listed albums in alphabetical order. If I was first on the list, the fans might check my name off before they got to the bottom of the list.

John P. Kee Surprises Me Onstage

John is often called the Crown Prince of Gospel, and rightfully so. He is a remarkable talent who reminds me of the work of such artists as Andrae Crouch and the Hawkins family.

I remember meeting John and his New Life Chorale for the first time in the 1980s. Initially, I didn't pay him that much attention even though he was getting good airplay and was building a following across the country. I hadn't seen him perform personally, so I wasn't aware of his great potential and what he had to offer musically. I must admit it took a little while for me to appreciate him.

So when he arrived at the WSMV studio in Nashville where I was taping my show at the time, I didn't pay any particular attention to him. To me, he was just another gospel artist and his choir was just another gospel choir—although I knew how popular they were.

John did a song that day that everyone who listened to it enjoyed. His choir exhibited a great deal of maturity and commitment to their leader. Even though John's choir has changed members over the years, they always keep that trademark John Kee sound.

I remember that when I aired him on my show, it got a good response from the audience. I've kept my eye on John from that time on, expecting great things from him, and he hasn't disappointed me yet. Over the years I've especially noticed that he is building an audience that extends beyond gospel-music fans. Everyone seems to love his music and style of performing.

By the time he appeared on my show again, I was doing live performances and I was glad to have him as a guest. Each time he would come to the stage the audience would just go berserk. He was a big draw.

John and I had the opportunity to spend a little time together. I learned that he likes sports—especially basketball. Although he's a warm and very friendly type of guy, he had a cadre of people around him that would keep people away from him.

John told me that he came from a big family—fourteen or fifteen kids—and that he had once been involved in drug activity in Charlotte, North Carolina. He talked about having worked out of a grocery store selling drugs, and how after the death of a close friend he saw the light, and felt that the Lord saved him from suffering the same fate.

"I was seeing young men dying on the streets, and I think it was then that I just made up my mind that I did not want to leave here like that. I didn't want to die on the streets," John told me one evening. He went on to relate how he had changed his lifestyle of drugs, easy money, and getting high. He said that he had prayed and made a "new covenant with God. I came to the Lord and He was ready to receive me."

We also talked about the positive work he was now doing in the community where he once had sold drugs, and about all the other different projects that he was involved with.

In our conversations, John would always talk a lot about his drug days. He also revealed that part of his past to his audiences. He wanted young people to know that they could be in that situation and still come out of it in a positive way and make a contribution to society. He said that it all depended on self-discipline and willpower.

John's middle name is Prince, and everybody started calling him the Prince of Gospel Music. James Cleveland was "the King," and Albertina Walker is still "the Queen." We have our own royal family in gospel music.

It was in the 1990s that John really established himself on the music scene. It was at the end of the big surge for the Winans. The Winans did their last popular recording when John's career started to mushroom, and he became the new superstar.

But even back when I first got to know him there were signs and indications that John Key was going to make an indelible impression on gospel music. He was developing a style that was distinctively his own, and it was interesting to watch him grow. John has always been a great artist, keyboard player, arranger, and producer. His talents run the whole gamut of the musical scene.

I think that what helped make John successful, besides his natural vocal ability, is that he pulled in so many different kinds of personalities from the community for his choir—much as I had done in my early Nashville days. His choir members were disciplined and involved in Christian activities. This was kind of unusual for tough young kids from the ghetto, and it caught a lot of people's attention.

Then John started doing something that was very unusual. He began giving away money at his concerts. I don't know why he did that—I never asked him. I assume he felt he was blessed and wanted to share his good fortune. He would just pick someone out from the audience—a complete stranger—and give them money. People really started to pack his concerts, hoping that they would be the ones to walk away a little richer.

Believe it or not, I was one of those lucky people. We were doing one of our live performances at the Nashville Auditorium, and John was there that night. In the middle of his performance he walked over to me and said, "I have a surprise for you."

His choir knew what was going to happen and they were kidding me. John called me to center stage and said, "Dr. Jones, this is seed money to help you expand your television ministry."

I was shocked. It was absolutely unbelievable. He gave me a check for five thousand dollars. This was the first time any artist had ever made a financial contribution to what I was trying to do on television. Nobody had ever done that for me. I didn't know whether to accept it or not.

In fact, I remember being a little embarrassed, because people always thought I had plenty of money. But that has not always been the case. At the time, our organization was struggling. That gesture endeared me to John more than ever.

Today I'm even more proud of him, because John has opened a church in Charlotte, North Carolina. They have a tremendous street ministry going there. It takes a brave soldier to go to the streets and talk about Jesus.

The Whole Drug Scene Saddens Me

Talking about John P. Kee and the problems he once had with drugs makes me reflect on the whole drug scene that's going on today in African-American communities all across America.

It saddens me to see our young people having to use mind-altering substances to make sense out of life. It indicates how sick our society is—for both blacks and whites—that we get drawn into using this kind of stuff. I don't believe it's a weakness of mentality that causes our kids to use drugs. I think that, instead, it's a desire to escape from unhappy situations and associations.

Whatever the real reasons, it appears that a large percentage of our young black people are caught and trapped into using drugs. I have never experimented with drugs. I've never even seen what cocaine looks like, and you'd think that at my age and with all my show-business experience, that I would have been in the presence of it.

Cocaine—especially crack—is an extremely devastating drug that was introduced into our communities across the nation in the 1980s, and was quickly absorbed by young people and the black population as a whole.

I remember reading a book called *The Godfather*, before I had any idea of what cocaine was all about and the influences and effects that it could have on one's life. In one of the chapters, a Mafia don says to his pals: "Let's dump these drugs into the black community—they'll use them." I think the Mafia must have had some reason to use drugs in our communities to divide our people, but I'm not exactly sure why.

What I mostly wonder about is, what is the attraction for drugs among our black youth? There are other minority groups who are deprived and poor but did not pick up the drug habit wholesale the way our people did. These other groups may have other habits that are just as bad, but it's curious as to why our black youth became so enchanted with cocaine. And why would anybody want to plant it in a community of people, knowing that it had the potential to become a disaster for that community? It just doesn't make any sense to me!

It also doesn't make any sense to me why we haven't done more to control distribution of these illegal substances from other countries. I think that if the federal government really wanted to stop drugs from being brought in, it certainly could. I don't think we'll ever be able to stop drug trafficking altogether, because people will always find a way to get what they want. But I certainly think that the government can do more in terms of establishing tighter controls.

When I do my show, I'm constantly talking about some of the challenges that black people face out there, and how we need to effect positive changes. I don't specifically pinpoint the drug-abuse situation; I also include coffee, cigarettes, alcohol, and other harmful things we consume that may be legal but nonetheless have a damaging effect on our bodies.

Like John Kee, I also believe that you can change any negative situation through discipline. When you have no discipline you begin to destroy yourself and others around you. And that even applies to coffee drinking! If you don't discipline yourself and you drink too much coffee—which *is* addictive—it can be detrimental not only to your own good health, but also can have a detrimental effect on others because of the personality changes that a lack of caffeine may cause. The same thing applies to alcohol or cocaine or marijuana: any one of these substances can alter our personalities and our behavior.

18

Marriage Was Not in the Stars

I t was during this period that I was trying to decide whether I was going to get married or stay a bachelor. I was dating a young woman from Nashville by the name of Jean Davidson. We had been seeing each other for a number of years, going back to the time when I was working for McGraw-Hill. Jean was a nurse, and I first met her at a church function. She was singing in her church choir and I was singing with the Royal Gospel Singers in Nashville at the time.

A couple of guys in my group were in relationships with some of the young ladies in Jean's group, and that's how I was eventually introduced to her. I think she fell in love with me right away, and I accepted her love.

She was a very attractive young woman, quite intelligent, and a good friend. Jean was someone I cared an awful lot about. She had never been married, either, and both of us were getting up in age. I know she wanted some kind of resolution to our relationship. I think she was always trying to say that to me in some way—"Are we going to do this or are we just going to remain friends or what?"

I loved her and I know she loved me. But at the time, I didn't feel moved to make that commitment. I don't know all the reasons why— so many of them were on a subconscious level. Coming from the kind of family that I did, commitment to personal relationships was always something of a problem for me. I just knew I didn't want to get married.

So I examined the situation in every direction to see if this was someone I wanted to commit my life to and do all the things that follow when you get married. I finally came to the conclusion that marriage was not in our future, but friendship certainly was.

I don't know whether I regretted it or not, or if I just felt that I was not intended to be married at this point. Twenty years later I would find the woman I wanted to marry. In the meantime, I went on to do what I did, and Jean and I remained good friends.

Lord, I'm a Travelin' Man

In the late 1980s I had stopped recording any more albums because I was still disappointed over the botched release of my 1986 album, *Another Time*. So it was a long time out of the recording studio until my next effort, in 1990, when I released *I'll Never Forget* on Malaco Records. This record did somewhat better than my last one had.

Throughout most of this period and into the early 1990s I was kept busy traveling between Nashville and Washington, D.C., where BET's production studios are located. I edited my show there.

On the flights between Nashville and Washington I got to meet some interesting people—mainly politicians—because I was flying first-class back and forth. One of the people I met was Michael Espy, who was the first black Secretary of Agriculture.

In some ways these flights were like a mini-ministry because I'd always be talking to these politicians about gospel music. And I was surprised how many of these secular politicians were familiar with this type of music.

I was also staying busy doing a lot of traveling and performing around the country in places like Alaska, which was a very interesting place to visit. I had always wanted to see that part of the country, because it's such an isolated area.

I got my opportunity to do so one February when I arrived in Anchorage with a couple of other gospel singers. However, it was so cold that we didn't see much of the city or anything else. Mostly we put on our boots and walked around where the hotel was located.

We stayed there for four or five days and performed for an auditorium filled with black people, which somewhat surprised me. I learned that they were the families of former U.S. soldiers who had served on the base there and decided to remain. I never knew before I arrived that there were so many blacks living in Anchorage.

Besides traveling to places like Alaska, I was also doing some performing with Barbara Mandrell in Las Vegas and other cities. In addition, I was doing a lot of traveling overseas. We were performing in countries such as England, Holland, France, Germany, and Israel.

In England, where I arrived to host a gospel show, I was amazed by the caliber of black gospel artists they had in that country. There was some great talent. But what surprised me most was that the British gospel artists had very little knowledge of traditional gospel music or the history of African-American gospel music. They told me they didn't follow America's traditional style of gospel music at all. They were all into the Winans and Kirk Franklin—contemporary gospel artists like that; but being as formal as British blacks are, I had thought they'd know more about traditional gospel music.

Germany was also interesting to me. I'd been to that country a few times before, starting back in the 1980s, after my first visit to Holland. What always surprised me was the large number of Africans I saw living in Germany. With all the hatred that the Germans have traditionally felt toward Jews and blacks, I thought that I would suffer, being there. But on the two occasions I've been there, the people paid no special attention to us. They were used to seeing blacks. What they were thinking about us inside, however, is an entirely different story.

On the last visit to Germany, we went to a relatively remote area. I can't remember the name of the place, but it wasn't one of the great big cities. And when we went into stores to shop, I thought for sure we'd be getting glares and stares and things like that. But that never happened and it was a learning experience for me. Even here we saw a lot of Africans. It was really a trip!

I guess the times I've been to Germany I always kind of had in the back of my mind the things these people used to say about blacks and Jews, during the Nazi era. But we were there on a Christian mission, and we didn't get into any discussions about racial or ethnic issues. And once I saw that we were not going to be an anomaly in that country, I stopped worrying about us being under the spotlight and maybe experiencing some hostility. The treatment of us there was normal.

Going to these countries gave me important life lessons, because these experiences continued to sensitize me to various people in the world and their needs.

Worries on My Mind

Although this was an interesting period, and despite the pleasure of doing all this performing around the world, I was not entirely free of anxiety. Because of the insecurities I have suffered most of my life, I was always anxious about whether BET would renew my contract or not.

I had watched some other shows and other personalities on the BET network come and go, and I knew how quickly things can happen in the television business. So I was always worried about some crisis situation taking place and that I would be forced to stop doing what I loved so much. I wanted to be prepared in case that happened to me.

But, fortunately, I was able to work through all those years without interruption. And if you tune in your television set to my show this weekend, guess who will be there to greet you?

Minister Farrakhan Buys Me a Bottle of Cologne

I can't begin to tell you how awestruck I was on that day in 1987 when the phone rang at home. On the other end of the line was Minister Louis Farrakhan. He said he wanted to appear on my show which he watched regularly.

Of course, I told him he could, because I knew it would focus a lot of national media attention on my program. But after hanging up the phone I wondered what he could possibly do. After all, this was a Christian-music show, and Minister Farrakhan was a devout Muslim. I didn't know at the time that he was also a professional violinist.

I also decided to call Bob Johnson, the president of the BET network. I knew there was a lot of controversy about Farrakhan, and I had better let my boss know about this request. I was kind of in shock when Mr. Johnson said no to Minister Farrakhan's appearance. I worried about how I was going to tell Minister Farrakhan that he couldn't do the show when I had already told him that he could.

When I called Minister Farrakhan back and told him what Mr. Johnson had said, that was the end of that. The following week I had to go to New Orleans for a Gospel Music Workshop of America convention.

That very morning my phone rang, and Bob Johnson was on the other line. He said, "Bobby, that matter about Farrakhan. I've reconsidered and I guess we can let him do the show." I hung up wondering what was going on.

A couple of days later Minister Farrakhan called me again. He told me that an arrangement had been worked out where he wouldn't be interviewed on my show, but would stick to his violin playing, instead. That's when I learned he was a classically-trained violinist.

Well, Minister Farrakhan eventually arrived in Nashville. I hadn't notified Channel 4, whose studio I was using to tape my show, that this controversial figure was going to show up. Minister Farrakhan's security people arrived first, and they literally took over the studio. They wouldn't even let people up to the top of the hill where the station was located. They had Nation of Islam guards in the middle of the street.

I think there was some kind of standoff between this major NBC affiliate and the Farrakhan people. But some kind of compromise was worked out where NBC didn't cancel the taping, in return for an exclusive interview with the minister. So a potentially violent situation was defused.

When I showed up for the taping I had no idea what was going on. I didn't know that the whole studio had been taken over by Minister Farrakhan's people, so there I was walking right up to the front door. I could've gotten into some serious trouble, myself. Instead, I got escorted into the studio the back way.

Then we taped his segment. It was an incredible experience. Here I was singing "Amazing Grace" with a Muslim on a Christian television show, while he played his violin. I couldn't help but wonder how I was going to be perceived by the Christian community.

After he performed, we talked on the air, but it wasn't an interview format. Minister Farrakhan said a few things about Jesus. He said he perceived Jesus as a prophet. Nothing he said was offensive to anyone in my audience.

I remember that all his Muslim ladies were there and they hung on to every word he uttered. It was a good moment and it established a relationship between us.

Since then, I've been with him at several of his media-gathering events. I guess it has always puzzled people—especially the Nashville community—as to why I associate with him.

I do so because I like him. I like what he has to say to encourage our people, and what he has done for a lot of the derelicts in the black community. I see him differently than how he is perceived by white people. And he respects me. He feels that my medium for reaching black people is an excellent one.

With all due respect to some of my Jewish friends who believe otherwise, I feel that much of what Minister Farrakhan has said about the Jews over the years has been taken out of context. Talking to him, I simply do not get the impression that he is anti-Semitic.

I also believe that he has the right to believe what he wants to as far as his faith goes. I'm not going to embrace Islam, because I'm embracing Christianity, but I certainly respect all people of the Islamic persuasion.

I think that instead of being opposed to each other, as African-Americans we should develop more unified interpersonal relationships. African-American Christians should embrace African-American Muslims. It's only by being unified that we can stop anyone from trying to divide us and move forward as a race of people.

There was one day when Minister Farrakhan was in Nashville that I will never forget. He was staying at the Renaissance Hotel. He told me he wanted to go shopping, and that he wanted me to accompany him. So we decided to go to the Bellevue Shopping Mall. He wanted to buy some white shirts. He also told his security people that he wanted to spend some time with me alone.

Well, I have this little red Mercedes-Benz 190 and here we are heading down the interstate. I punched in my gospel music on my tape deck, and Minister Farrakhan is clapping along with the music, celebrating and enjoying it. It was kind of incredible.

And we just were having guy-to-guy talk. I thought that he had a very intriguing personality. So, for security reasons, we went in through the back entrance of this men's store, and the buzz was all over the mall like crazy—"Farrakhan is here."

We had a fun time shopping together. It was kind of strange to be shopping with a man of his stature. But we only went into one store, and we spent about an hour there. He even checked out some of the bow ties, which he always wears.

I ended up buying him the shirts—they were the best-quality white shirts—and in return he bought me a bottle of Obsession, a cologne. It's his favorite brand.

Then we got into my car—his bodyguards were following us—and I drove him back to his hotel. We had a chance to talk some more, and he talked about issues that could help our people.

At one point Minister Farrakhan made an interesting statement to me. He said he thought God was keeping me in my present situation instead of turning me into a blown-up personality because it was the most effective way for me to be helping black people.

Two Awards I Cherish More Than My Grammy

I received two honors in 1987 that—even today—still mean more to me than anything else in my life, including the Grammy. One was from gospel-music pioneer Sallie Martin, and the other was the Thomas A. Dorsey Award of Excellence.

Both of these people helped to create today's gospel-music sound and helped foster its popularity. Without gospel music, I wouldn't have had a career. How much closer can you get to the heart of what you do than earning honors such as these?

When I received the Thomas A. Dorsey Award at the organization's annual convention, I was quite blown away and elated by the honor, because I knew what it represented. It was an incredible jolt of support for someone like myself who felt like he was still just starting out in the business rather than being an accomplished veteran.

Sallie Martin gave me her award on my show. She had someone draw it up and it looks kind of hand-done. It is very personal and includes a picture of her. That's what makes it even more special. After having read as much as I can about the history of gospel music and the role she played in it with Thomas A. Dorsey, what an honor this award was for me! I remember feeling so joyous that day.

LaShun Pace and the Tennessee State Prison for Women

I was producing more live shows than ever before now, and still thinking about ways to expand *Bobby Jones Gospel*—something I eventually did in 1989 when I debuted *Video Gospel*. This new show was a half-hour gospel program that featured top videos from major Christian music artists.

That year—1987—I also met one incredible woman! Her name is LaShun Pace. She was singing with her sisters—they were known as the Pace Sisters—at the time. They were all full-figured girls from the state of Georgia who excelled at matched harmonies. I had heard a lot about them, and even my friend Albertina Walker had mentioned them to me. She was trying to compare them with another great gospel group, the Clark Sisters.

When I saw LaShun perform, I thought to myself: *Here's another Mahalia Jackson.* She was phenomenal in her ability to perform gospel music, and I sensed that her Mahalia Jackson persona was going to catapult her into the year 2000 in a unique way.

I got to know LaShun and her sisters very well. One day we did a show at the Tennessee State Prison for Women—we did it for BET. I decided to do that kind of show because I once saw Tammy Faye Bakker—she is the former wife of evangelist Jim Bakker—go into a prison setting and telecast live from there.

I remember being impressed by how Tammy handled herself in that environment, and I could see what her performance there meant to the inmates. So here I was in a prison with the Pace Sisters and one or two other artists who accompanied us.

It felt very strange being inside a prison. If it had been a men's prison, I would have been very apprehensive. But these were all women and I didn't have any fear being among them.

Once the concert began, I can still remember how receptive these women prisoners were to our performance. Many of them knew who we were even before we got there. We had a wonderful rapport and dialogue with these ladies.

What we brought these inmates was joy; I also believe we gave them some inspiration. The event was televised, so these prisoners' relatives even got a chance to see their kin on television. All in all, it was a worthwhile experience.

Afterward, I took the Pace Sisters out to dinner and one of the sisters—June—really liked the belt that I was wearing. I gave it to her as a gift, and June thought it was the greatest thing that could have happened. As a result, we became good friends and I still have a good relationship with her.

LaShun eventually went on to sing independently. And my relationship with her remains as personal as one can get in this business. We don't talk much on the phone, but when we see each other it's always very cordial.

I recall that my first impression of her—besides recognizing that she had an amazing voice—was that she was very shy. LaShun has a lot of insecurities because of her weight, and I can understand that. I was also impressed by her testimony and how she has come through the difficult days of her divorce. LaShun recently shared with me her experiences with her ex-husband, and how that divorce almost led her to suicide.

She even disclosed how she had once thought about killing herself while pregnant with her second child—that story also appears in my book *Touched by God*.

Offstage, LaShun is a very spiritual woman. Church fills most of her life. She prays early in the morning and she prays late at night. She is always trying to help people through their problems and she has always been very supportive of me.

The Reverend Lawrence Roberts

Around that same time, I also had the opportunity to meet another pioneer of gospel music, the Reverend Lawrence Roberts. He was the one who discovered Mahalia Jackson.

I had long wanted to meet him. Reverend Lawrence was instrumental in performing with and recording many of the gospel-music singers back in the early 1950s. He and his church choir were from Nutley, New Jersey. Reverend Roberts was producing for the Savoy record label back then, while still serving as pastor of his First Baptist Church. One of his first recordings for Savoy was with the Reverend James Cleveland. I remember that one song was called "Peace Be Still." I think that recording was the first time I ever heard of Reverend Cleveland.

Reverend Lawrence was also the first person to record Mahalia Jackson, so his influence in the gospel-music industry has been very profound. When I finally caught up with him at one of the gospel-music conventions, I invited him to appear on my show. This was during a period of time when I was doing my shows in concert halls and major arenas.

So he came and participated, and he also joined my advisory board; he and another guy, the bishop Jeff Banks, who was also a very well known character in the gospel-music industry, both became members of my board. They both would travel to Nashville to participate in what we were doing. Bishop Banks also had a big choir and did real well with his group. I was very pleased to get both of these men to become so active in my organization. These men kept the traditional element of gospel music alive and, as you know, that means an awful lot to me.

Reverend Roberts is now living in Atlanta. He called me recently to let me know that he came into a lot of money. He said that a famous family had left him a million dollars. I don't quite remember how he met this family, but he was doing something for them in some way and that impressed them. They liked him. So they gave him an endowment.

Over the years Reverend Lawrence has helped a lot of people around him, and he has also suffered some personal tragedy. I remember that his son—he was a very handsome guy—was shot in some kind of robbery attempt on him and was blinded.

After that terrible tragedy, Reverend Roberts went through some years struggling with depression. When he got the money from this family, he was able to bring his son with him to Georgia and take proper care of him. That money was a blessing from God.

20

An Explosion of Gospel Music

One morning I got a phone call from a woman named Joanne Berry, who was Barbara Mandrell's manager. As I've already said, Barbara loved black gospel music, and Joanne wanted to produce a black gospel-music show in Nashville. Joanne wanted top names to appear in the show. She had contacted the Reverend Milton Brunson, the Thompson Community Singers, the Clark Sisters, Shirley Caesar, the Mighty Clouds of Joy, Cissy Houston, and my New Life Singers.

Barbara didn't plan to be there, so Joanne asked me if I would host the show. "Of course," I told her. I would be pleased to do it. So all of these stars came to Nashville. They set up at one of our major outdoor amphitheaters, which is called the Starwood Theater.

We were all trying to think what we should call the event, and we came up with the name *The Gospel Explosion*. And that's how the name for the Bobby Jones Gospel Explosions, which I produce two or three times a year, came into being.

Well, the week before the show it rained almost every day. It was just like the sky had opened up over Nashville and refused to close. That Saturday we had a pre-show rehearsal, and I thought that by the evening things would lighten up a little. It did not.

It rained cats and dogs. Sunday, the day of the show, it was still raining. Sunday afternoon, it still poured. We knew people weren't going to show up in this kind of weather. In fact, ticket sales were poor. Fortunately, it wasn't my money!

We got to the theater and the pouring rain continued. We anticipated a completely empty house. But believe it or not, at six o'clock, the exact time the show was scheduled to begin, the sun came out, and four thousand people turned out to watch us.

It was magnificent! My singers and I performed the song, "I'm So Glad I'm Standing Here Today," for which Barbara and I had won the Grammy.

That show was also the inspiration for me to do live, out-of-studio programs. It was something I had long been thinking about doing anyway, but this was the initiative for me to get it started. I remember asking my friend Al Hobbs, and my cousin Delores Poindexter, to tell me what they thought about this kind of out-of-studio entertainment. They saw the show and they encouraged me to do more of these.

I think the first one I did was at Nashville's War Memorial Auditorium. It was a place I could easily afford. I had a bunch of artists come in and it did very well. It was a two-day taping, and by the time it was through, I had enough material for several shows on my television program. Eventually I expanded the taping to four days.

Now I no longer had to be concerned about taping my shows in studios. I could do it all at once at one of these Explosions. By the third year, the Gospel Explosions had become so successful, that I moved the tapings to the Tennessee Performing Arts Center. Now all the major gospel record labels began sending me their artists so that I could promote them.

It kept on mushrooming. I even had a Youth Explosion. We would invite young church choirs and young artists; these shows, we did in July, when school was out.

I'll never forget building my first set on one of these Explosions. I was able to contact some people who worked at Opryland, and they sent me several pieces. With these props we were able to make the stage look nice.

We used only three cameras to shoot the Explosions. I thought the professional quality of these programs was kind of embarrassing. But, fortunately, my audiences didn't take notice.

These Explosions were an experiment, and the good thing was that my ratings didn't drop. I remember that Mr. Johnson, who owned BET, didn't particularly care for these kinds of shows. He preferred that we shoot my gospel show in a studio because there was a cleaner look and better sound than with these live performances. I didn't have all the whistles and bells back then to give these out-of-studio productions that kind of look. But as I said, my ratings stayed high so he didn't really bother me. Had they dropped, I'm sure he would have encouraged me to quickly get back into the studio.

So that's the story of how my Gospel Explosions got started.

I Call It Quits with My New Life Singers

I hadn't been in a recording studio since the release of *Another Time*, in 1986. My albums weren't selling all that well, and nobody was rushing to sign us up. So when Malaco Records approached me in 1990, I was very delighted to find a record company who wanted to record us. It's a proven fact that those people who both have television shows and are singers, don't sell many records. As I said earlier, people identify you with either one or the other—but not both.

But Malaco Records decided to take a chance with us. I think they thought, with me having a television show, it would open up a lot of avenues for them—which it really did. So they recorded us in this little town called Muscle Shoals, Alabama.

I went down there with six girls, and I chose some material that I thought would be a good representation of me and my New Life group. We went into that studio and it took us two days to finish up.

When I finished, I was a little anxious about the project. I was hoping it would do better than my other albums. I had a history of not being able to sell album projects, regardless if it was me leading the project, or one of my group. So this time I put enough voices on the album to make sure that if it didn't sell, I wouldn't be the only reason for it not being successful. Still, the album didn't do that well, and that was another disappointment for me. Nowadays I think its lack of success had more to do with the way the record label marketed us than the talent and the material.

Then, in 1994, I did a live album at one of my gospel Explosions at the Tennessee Performing Arts Center. It was called *Bring It to Jesus*. It was recorded on the Tyscot label after I had asked Malaco Records to release me from my contract. I went with this new record company because they had promised they'd give me my own label, which never happened.

But this turned out to be a much, much better received album. I had some great singers on it, like Beverly Crawford, and the album gained a lot more recognition than some of the other albums I had done.

Ultimately, that whole project resulted in a very disappointing time for me. It was such a great recording, that I just knew it was going to put us in the mainstream. In fact, Sparrow Records wanted to pick this album up; but that deal fell apart because of the girls in New Life. Here I was on a quest to try and provide these young singers with an opportunity to further their careers, and they jeopardized the whole process.

After Sparrow indicated interest in picking up the album, my singers got hold of this young lawyer and came back with all kinds of demands. They were demanding a part of my TV show, and eighty percent of the proceeds off album sales. They wanted the rights to the New Life name, which was, of course, protected. All of this really came from the young attorney that they had hired. But this aggressive attitude made me feel very uncomfortable.

So I decided to disband the group. I had had these warm feelings for them and they had showed nothing but a lack of confidence in me.

It was a very disturbing time. I went through a long period of feeling very bad about that situation. If there was any bright spot, it was that Beverly Crawford, who was the lead singer of that entity, did not join in the revolt. She stayed loyal to me, which didn't give the rest of the singers the leverage that they thought they had.

The action of my singers was yet another time in my life when I felt betrayed. I just think that many people who worked for me came in for the wrong reasons—or, at least, they hadn't come in for the reasons I wanted them to work for me.

I was looking at these young singers, for example, as new artists to whom I was giving an opportunity to expose their talents. I was offering them hard-to-find experience in the record industry. And they were thinking that I was making a ton of money—which I wasn't—and that I wasn't sharing that money equally with them.

My position was that I had a pay scale like anyone else, and like any employees, you paid them what their job called for. And that's what I did. Which was fair. But they had this other idea in their heads, that I was making more money and not taking care of them. It was like they wanted to be living in mansions, driving big cars, and things like that, and they were just starting out.

This whole experience taught me not to have any high expectations of people I work with. Because even with the ones who I thought were a little more into the seriousness of what they were doing, their reactions to many situations allowed me to see that they were not always Divinely guided.

And that was kind of heartbreaking to me. Especially later on, when I saw that even Beverly Crawford, who had remained loyal to me, and whom I really trusted a lot, made some decisions and took some actions which I felt were certainly out of order.

What happened with Beverly is that just before she had a child, this record label had approached her with an offer. Of course I wanted that for her, but I expected that label to come to me first. After all, I was the one who had groomed her, and brought her in, and presented her to the country. So I thought this label would at least say something about it to me—but they didn't!

And the way they handled that whole recording situation was offensive. I wasn't included in any of the aspects of what was happening. I was loyal to Beverly, and she went ahead and left me out of the whole process.

21

I Baptize Al Gore's Wife

It seems that most of my adventures begin with a phone call. This one was no different—on the other end of the line was an aide from then senator Al Gore's office. It was 1991, and Mr. Gore had decided to make a bid for a higher office—and ultimately became Bill Clinton's vice president. To publicize his decision to run for the presidency, Senator Gore wanted to go on a fact-finding tour of Israel. The senator's aide explained to me that Mr. Gore wanted to take along some Nashville gospel musicians, along with members of the city's Jewish community.

So there I was—one of three blacks among a contingent of forty-four of the city's most prominent Jewish leaders. This was my fourth trip to Israel, but this time I was traveling with Senator Albert Gore. I was part of a high-level U.S. Government visit, so the treatment I received on this trip was even more special than when I did the film for the Israeli tourism board. You can imagine how I felt, being a token black man among a plane full of Southern Jews. But I was pleased that the Jewish contingent embraced me as if I were truly one of their own.

There are some special things that happened on this trip, all of them reflecting the blessings I've always received from the Lord. One of those special moments was serving as the honor bearer in a ceremony at the Holocaust Museum. Israeli troops showed up at this ceremony to pay special tribute to the victims of Nazi atrocities. I was very moved, but also slightly embarrassed. It seemed a little strange for me to be given this honor, since I wasn't even Jewish. But I was among those who had been selected. We had to take the wreath and, along with the senator, place it in a certain area. So I played a major part in this touching ceremony.

Then Senator Gore and Tipper Gore, his wife, took us all along with them to the Syrian border. He was observing the situation, and the Israelis were filling him in on things. I remember that the Zionists were talking to the senator about the problems they were having with the Orthodox Jews. It was very interesting to hear all this.

I think the highlight of the trip was when we went to the Jordan River. It was a beautiful day when we arrived there. I remember that the river was not very clear; it was a little bit on the brown side. But there we were—all forty-five of us. So we got off the bus and walked toward the river with much reverence. That's the river in which John baptized Jesus. It's a sacred site, and for us Christians, one of the holiest sites in Israel.

We approached the Jordan, and the guide was giving us the history of the river. He was telling us how during certain months, the river overflows and fertilizes the fields in the area. Then he asked if any of us would like to be baptized in that river. And some of us who weren't Jewish, did. The Gores and I decided to get baptized. So the guide gave us some water from the river.

I've been in church long enough to know what words to say: "In the name of the Father, the Son, and the Holy Ghost. In remembrance of our Savior, Jesus Christ . . ."

Tipper allowed me to baptize her. She knew I was a gospel singer. I think I asked her if she would allow me to do so. And I poured an entire bottle of Jordan River water, not directly on her head, but over the back of her blonde hair. And then I allowed Senator Gore to baptize me.

To this very day I think this is a very special thing to have happened to me. Not only for a black man to baptize a senator's wife, but, in return, to be baptized by a future vice president of the United States.

. . .

$\mathcal{W}$e left the Jordan and I had a chance to sing to the group on the bus. I did a gospel version of "My Country 'Tis of Thee," and they just melted. There was a special bonding between everyone on that trip.

I also suspect it was as a result of this trip, that when the senator became vice president of the United States, I was among many other Tennessee representatives who were invited to the inauguration.

New Life and I had a chance to perform at the Tennessee Pavilion for the vice president. I chatted with him backstage and we recalled our trip to Israel together. There were a lot of luminaries who appeared during that program, including country-music star Ricky Skaggs. Later that evening, I had a chance to visit Mr. Gore's home.

Since then, I've visited with the Gores on other occasions. I got invited to one of the vice president's receptions in his Washington, D.C., home in 1998, and the year before that we performed for Mr. and Mrs. Gore at a picnic at the Hermitage in Nashville. I still have photographs of the New Life Singers dancing with the vice president and his wife.

I know you're going to laugh, but one of the girls from my group—Emily—was dancing with the vice president and pinched him on his butt. I told her she could be put in jail for that, but she said it was worth having taken the chance. "He was dressed in jeans and I just wanted to feel his butt," she told me.

The vice president did not have her arrested; instead, he just laughed because it was all done in fun. He's a very personable man—just like you see him on TV. But although he's fun-loving, he can be serious at times.

He loves his children, and is very much like his father, who was also a senator from the state of Tennessee. My mother was very fond of his father, and blacks, in general, really liked Senator Gore Senior.

Today, I very much support Vice President Gore politically. I'm politically active. I am a fighter for human rights and for any cause that provides for human rights and decency among all people of the world. That's why I had made that dangerous trip to South Africa. It was to make up for not having participated in the civil-rights movement as far as the marching and sit-ins were concerned.

All the years that I've been in Nashville, I've done concerts and worked on different programs that would enhance the community— like Project Help. Even now I'm in the process of raising two million dollars for Tennessee State University because they are going to name the performing-arts center in my honor.

These are some of the ways that I help—ways that I've always helped—to encourage decency and try to bring about positive change in this troubled world of ours.

22

My Soul Mate, at Last!

I first met Ethel Williams in 1992. She had come to one of my live Explosions. She was a pretty lady. She brought her daughter, Sonnetta, who was Miss Black Georgia. Ethel had been a schoolteacher and now worked as principal of a school in Augusta, Georgia. The following year she again appeared at one of my Explosions, this time with her husband.

I thought I needed a board at the time. I was modeling my organization after James Cleveland's Gospel Music Workshops of America. So I liked the two of them enough to ask them to join my board.

As I mentioned earlier, my growing organization was a threat to Reverend Cleveland. He started looking at me differently. He saw something in me and my TV show that was somehow alarming to him.

I'll never forget that Reverend Cleveland would send one of his people to scout me out. He would stand around backstage and watch everything I was doing and report back to his boss, which I disliked very much. It created a little friction between us.

Meanwhile Ethel and her husband had gotten divorced. But she became an active board member and began to frequent all of the Explosions. Then, in 1996, it became evident that she was becoming interested in me. And I was in need of someone being interested in me. Well, that eventually turned into a relationship.

We started dating in July 1996. After my mother passed away in

1997, we deepened our commitment to each other. We sealed that commitment in a one-on-one ceremony and she has been my mate ever since.

I know that you probably have many questions about our marriage. And you know, from reading this book, that I'm a very open person about my life. But some things are precious and are better kept private. So forgive me if I keep any further details about our relationship to myself.

BeBe, CeCe, and Some Jealousy Toward Oprah

I can't remember exactly when BeBe and CeCe came into the picture—I think it was sometime between 1991 and 1992. I had noticed them performing on the PTL (Praise The Lord) network, and they went on from there to produce their first major hits.

When their record label approached me to have them appear on my show, I was delighted. I was taping the show on Channel 4 at the time. I was back in the studio because I had run out of material for that year from my live Explosions.

So they came and did the show. I introduced them to the gospel marketplace and the song that they did, "Heaven," became a major hit. That song and their whole album was very successful for the two of them. It kicked off their careers. Before appearing on my program they had basically been exposed only to the contemporary Christian Music market.

CeCe offstage is just a doll—a genuinely warm person. The same goes for her brother. I've never spent a lot of time around them other than during performing situations, but I've always felt that I have a good relationship with both these artists. My attorney and good friend, Richard Manson, by the way, managed CeCe at the time.

It was CeCe who introduced me to Whitney Houston. Whitney, who is Cissy Houston's daughter, knew of me from my show. I don't think that in all my years on television, I have yet met a black entertainer of any major stature who has not watched my show. Some of these entertainers use it as their church. I'm no longer surprised when some star tells me that they tune in to my show on Sunday mornings and feel as if they are in church.

CeCe and BeBe's parents are very wonderful people as well. They're also singers, and I had them on my program. In fact, I recently recorded an album with CeCe's mother Delores; it's called *A Lifetime to Remember* and the orchestra is none other than the London Symphony Orchestra.

It was quite a massive project and I got to be good friends with the whole family—including CeCe's children, who are as positive as their mother. My only gripe—and maybe it goes back to the Grammy Award and their treatment of me back then—is that the Winans family as a group would never do my show.

I don't know why they have rejected us—several members of the family, including BeBe and CeCe, have already appeared on my program—but they do. Maybe it's because some of the people in their organization still harbor some sort of resentment against me. Or maybe they feel that *Bobby Jones Gospel* is not the kind of show they want to present themselves on. I even ran the Winans' family video on my *Video Gospel* show, but I've never been able to work things out with them.

It's interesting that despite all this, Marvin Winans' ex-wife has turned out to be one of my best friends. We're just inseparable and love each other. She's the one who told me that Marvin kept discouraging the whole family from appearing on my show.

It used to make me a little jealous to see the Winan's family performing on *Oprah*. It also used to make me feel a bit badly that Oprah never had me on her show. After all, she and I go back a long time. I knew her when she was just starting out, and the Winans didn't.

Perhaps the reason why Oprah had them on her show is because of their success in the secular-music field. It brought her show a lot of attention. But I think that Oprah is being disloyal to her own people by not having a black gospel-music performer like myself on her show.

I've never approached Oprah to talk to her about the situation. But a lot of people have often wondered why I never did her show, especially because of the kind of relationship we once had. After all, she once lived in Nashville and we used to party together. But I have never brought this up to her.

I've run into Oprah twice since she left Nashville and became a big star, and on one of those occasions I interviewed her for my show. This was during one of the Image Award productions, and I was there with a BET camera crew. She talked to me backstage about the good times we used to have together. She acted normal with me, but never once asked if I'd like to be on her show. As I've said, you just never know about people.

Yolanda Adams' Battle for Success

Yolanda is my tall, wonderful, and gorgeous friend. Over the years I've watched her rise from being a choir singer, to major status in the gospel-music realm. She is so pretty, with her model-like looks, that I must admit when I first met her sometime in 1992, I developed a slight crush. Nowadays she is married to Timothy Crawford, who was an Indianapolis Colts football player.

Yolanda started coming to some of my Explosions, and she didn't have a record label at that time. I began to give her a lot of airtime, and soon she was picked up by the Tribute record label. It was then she started to develop as a solo singer. So I'm pleased to have had a lot to do with her current success.

Yolanda is a special performer as far as I'm concerned. She stands very tall (and *is* very tall) in her ability to communicate her message to her audiences. She has crossover appeal, which I think is very good for us in this industry.

Another thing I like about Yolanda is that she has exposed gospel music to a huge secular audience through her appearances on *The Tonight Show with Jay Leno* and other television programs. With her great voice and impeccable wardrobe, she is a good model for what this industry can produce.

I've been backstage with Yolanda, been invited to her birthday parties, and even visited her home. She is a very sensitive girl and you really have to get to know her before she opens up to you. She doesn't open up to everybody.

She seems to be locked in a struggle with something out there, and I think that has impeded her progress as a star in some unconscious way. I have no clue at all as to what that struggle was all about. Maybe it had something to do with the fact that she was forced to take care of her family after her father died, and she had to look after her brothers and sisters. Maybe it had something to do with the fact that she was so tall growing up, and people didn't always view her height as something beautiful. Maybe she was taunted about her physical appearance as a youngster—just as I was.

23

Bonding with Kirk Franklin, and Awed by Aretha

I've introduced a lot of great gospel-music artists over the more than twenty-five years I've been in this wonderful business. One of the greatest contributions I've ever made was exposing the public for the first time to a young performer by the name of Kirk Franklin.

Little did I know, of course, when Vickie Mack Lataillade, president of then just-starting-up GospoCentric Records, first approached me in 1994 to get her talented new discovery on my show, that Kirk would become one of the most sought-after artists in this business.

We were taping my show in Atlanta, Georgia, that year. This was the first time we had moved the show to a different state for taping, so everything was a little different for us. I was quite busy. I had a full roster of artists booked for that show. In fact, I was overbooked.

I had known Vickie when she and I briefly worked together at Sparrow Records just before it folded. Since then, she had begun her own record company. It was good to see her after all those years and catch up. But when she said, "Bobby, please help me out because I need to get this young artist some exposure—he's one of my first new artists," I shook my head. I told her that I doubted I could get Kirk on because we were already so heavily booked.

I really didn't pay much attention to Vickie's request. Not only was

I in the midst of trying to schedule a lot of artists, but to me Kirk was just another guy who wanted to be on my show. Then I thought about it some more and decided to give this young performer a little time at the end of my show. I think I changed my mind because of how intently Vickie asked me to do so. I guess I'm like that. If there's a way I can help someone out—even by just making a little space on my show—I try to do it.

Needless to say, Kirk was a big hit. The audience just loved him. Watching him perform, I also thought he was pretty good. And as his album continued to get radio play, he got more and more response from gospel-music fans.

I did know a little bit about Kirk Franklin back then. I once saw him in Nashville playing keyboard with another choir called the Dallas–Fort Worth Choir. I had seen him another time playing keyboard with the Georgia Mass Choir. But I remember not paying much attention to him because he wasn't a singer—he couldn't sing. He was an arranger, writer, producer, and played a fine piano, but he had no singing voice. Kirk's not even a rapper, he just talks his way through.

I didn't know in those days that Kirk was from the black ghetto of Fort Worth, Texas, or that he had grown up a troubled, street-tough kid who was part of the gang culture. Neither did I know that he had been abandoned as a child by his teenaged mother, or how much his grandmother had sacrificed to pay for his music lessons and tried to keep him out of trouble. I think I might have paid more attention to him if I had.

But over the years I've gotten to know all that about Kirk, and more. I know, for example, how sensitive he is about his music—and that he feels stung by the criticism he receives for his hip-hop style of gospel music. I also know that he is an ordained minister and how important the Christian gospel-music arena is to him despite what his detractors might claim.

Whenever we have the opportunity to get together, Kirk treats me like his father. He calls me his "papa" out of love and respect for me.

And he acknowledges that I'm one of his mentors and someone who helped him along the way to become the star that he is today.

One of the ways Kirk shows me respect is by attending various functions that I sponsor, whenever he can. In return, I have invited him to various international gospel events that I've been involved in, like a festival in Barbados, West Indies.

I think the longest time we spent together was on a plane ride back from Los Angeles to Dallas. We sat together and both of us had intentions of going to sleep, but we didn't. In fact, we talked all night. He listened carefully and was very attentive. I talked about the industry and told him things that had happened before his time. I told him about a lot of my own experiences over the years.

In return, he told me all about his years growing up in Dallas. How when he was a kid people would taunt him and call him gay. And he told me all about how he used to smoke marijuana, drink lots of liquor, and about participating in gang activities so that he could fit in.

And I had a chance to tell him about my own life growing up in Henry and Paris, Tennessee, and how I suffered similar taunts and how much I also tried to fit in but never really could.

I tried to tell him things that might help him along his way. I talked to him about how to deal with people, and how to manage himself in the face of his many critics. I also told him to accept what the Lord had given him as far as his talents went.

Kirk told me that he had very positive feelings toward traditional gospel music and the artists who performed that kind of music. He said that he used to go to the Gospel Music Workshops of America where he would listen to this kind of music. He also said he never really had planned to perform the kind of music he was noted for today, with his hip-hop generation trademark look. It was just one of the things he tried as a youthful gospel artist in a competitive market.

"I just felt that Generation X didn't want to hear from the reverend behind the pulpit," he explained. "But I wanted to get the message of Jesus to them in another way. So this was one of the things I put out and these kids caught on to it and a lot of people enjoyed it. Sometimes you just put something out there and you never know if it's going to catch on or not. That's the way it is in life."

I grew to love this young artist on that plane ride. I think we bonded because he got to know more about me and I got to learn more about him. He told me how he maintains himself and doesn't let all his success go to his head.

Kirk and I also talked about some of his future plans, and I was impressed not only with his spirituality, but the fact that he was very much in love with his wife and children.

When he talked to me about how hurt he felt from all the criticism of his style of gospel music, I let him know that whenever you are in the front line of a battle, you're going to be the first one to catch a bullet. And that's where he was standing.

"Be grateful to God that He put you out there," I said. "God will give you what you need to sustain your battle with your enemies."

And I believe that. I believe that the Lord chose Kirk to continue to spread His word in this unorthodox manner throughout the world. I think he's on the front line of a new gospel army.

Throughout that plane ride I was trying to help ease his transition to stardom. There was no other way I could do it but by saying positive things. And they were the truth. Another truth is that Kirk Franklin is a very nice person and a well-intended person who believes in what he does.

Awed by Aretha

It was a chilly fall evening in New York City in 1997. There I was standing in the wings of the fabled Avery Fisher Hall, when something absolutely incredible happened to me.

Aretha Franklin was headlining the show for its two–day run, and my group, along with the Canton Spirituals, were among the other featured acts. I had first encountered the Canton Spirituals as a singing unit in 1995, and the truth is, they didn't impress me. I just didn't care about quartet singing. It wasn't one of my ultimate loves.

And I think the feeling was mutual. I had heard that they didn't like the way I did things, and didn't like my style of singing. They didn't care for the people who sang with me and things like that. This was all hearsay, of course, but things they were supposedly saying about me got back to me.

Those feelings changed when I finally invited the group to one of my retreats in Las Vegas. They were still singing with Harvey Watkins Sr., their father and their leader, who at the time had been diagnosed with cancer and was very sick. At this retreat, all of them got a chance to meet me and observe me firsthand, and I got a chance to know them better. I even learned to appreciate their approach to gospel music. We all had a spiritual good time and we all changed our opinions of each other.

I ran into the Canton Spirituals months later at Carnegie Hall, of all places, where we were backstage waiting for Aretha to finish her act. We had been invited to participate in this AIDS benefit with her. And who did she choose for the honor of closing her show, but my group.

Well, Harvey Watkins just couldn't understand that—he was fuming! How could I close the show over the Canton Spirituals who at the time were making such an impression in the gospel-music marketplace? He thought his group was the hottest thing out there. How could my ensemble be chosen to follow Aretha?

To tell you the truth, I think I felt the same way. No way were we in the same category popularity-wise as the Canton Spirituals. In any case, with Harvey Watkins and the Canton Spirituals gloomily standing there watching, we closed the show.

We were so good, Aretha came back onstage with us and performed an encore. It just turned the place upside down and Harvey didn't have a word to say. The next night the same thing happened. Our segment was so good that, again, Aretha came out to sing with us.

But the last night of her appearance, Aretha came out onstage to make a statement, that no matter how good we were, she was the queen bee, and musically better than any of us. Much to our surprise, she put on a whole new presentation for her closing. She wore a church hat and high heels, and had a symphony orchestra, a singing group, and a choir backing her up—all of that.

To this very day, I still think all that effort was a message to us that we should never try to outdo one of the greatest singing stars of all time. Back then, however, all I could think about was how awesome it was just being part of her show.

That night Cicely Tyson was a guest of hers, along with the Reverend Jesse Jackson. A lot of local New York City dignitaries were also in attendance. And despite that elaborate onstage statement to us, and even though most of the audience was white and had no idea who Bobby Jones and his New Life Singers were, Aretha had us finish up the show for her.

Well, afterward I was working up enough nerve to ask her why she had let us close the evening instead of the Canton Spirituals. Aretha had come to get me and I was thinking about this as we walked out of the building together. All the press people were snapping shots, and we were holding hands. I got into her limo, and she gave me the bag of money she had earned that evening to hold.

We were riding to the reception hall where she had planned this great dinner. Aretha told me that I would be sitting at the table with her. It made me feel so special that evening. It was an exhilarating experience. But there was still that one burning question I needed to ask her. Finally, I broached the question.

"Why'd you do that, Miss Franklin, have us close your show?"

She looked at me and smiled. "Oh, baby, 'cause you're the best."

That night after the reception I did a lot of thinking. *What kind of impression am I giving off?* I asked myself. Aretha Franklin calls us "the best," but we put out an album and we don't sell but fifty or sixty thousand copies. All the major stars tell us they want to perform with us because we're so good, but people don't buy our albums.

I must admit, that evening I felt pretty confused about exactly who I was and the difference in people's opinions about our talent as performers. All I could think of is that maybe being on TV was more of a detriment to my singing career than an asset. Maybe people had gotten used to me as a television entertainer rather than a singer.

The reception was unbelievable. I just couldn't believe I was sitting with Aretha Franklin. And in her generous manner she goes, "Oh, child, I can't believe I'm sitting with Bobby Jones."

I remember thinking that a year earlier I had experienced the same sense of exhilaration. Out of the blue Aretha had called me and I couldn't believe that it was her on the phone. After all, she was one of my idols. We chatted about doing things together in the future, and then she said: "I'm going to do this tour for AIDS. Do you and your singers want to be on this gospel program in Detroit?"

I was stunned and delighted. I couldn't get over the fact that Aretha Franklin knew about me and New Life and had picked up the phone to call. Without a second's hesitation I told her I would be pleased to participate.

We talked some more, and then I asked her if she would be interested in doing my show once she finished her tour. I was so nervous—I'm always shy about asking people of such magnitude to do my show. That's why I've never asked Oprah; I assume that if she wanted to do my show, her producers would call me and let me know. So I had to work up all my nerve to ask Aretha. And she said, "I'd love to do it." I couldn't believe it.

At our hotel in Detroit at the start of the AIDS tour, Aretha had a welcome basket waiting for me. I had only talked to her on the phone, and had never met her in person. Yet she was kind enough to do something like that.

Finally it was time for us to go to this church for rehearsal. It was the New Bethel Church, and Aretha's father, the Reverend C. L. Franklin, one of the most noted ministers in the world, was pastor there. Aretha was devoted to her dad, so going to his church was another adventure for us. Tragically, some years later her father was shot and wounded during a robbery, and Reverend Franklin died as a result of those wounds.

At the church we did a sound check. Down the center aisle, directing things, was Aretha herself. We sat down and waited until she was through talking to her people and then we sort of eased down to her. She was very nonchalant.

"Hi," she said. "I'm glad to see you, and thanks for coming."

I didn't know what else to do, so I embraced her. And then I looked at her for some moments and she said, "What is it?"

"I'm just so glad to see you," I blurted out. "Darling, you've been an idol of mine. I've been watching you for years." I was feeling very emotional. Then I thought, *Let me get myself together because we have to do a performance. I have to impress her.*

Well, we're doing another sound check and she had just given us the schedule of performances for the benefit. I think we were going to be about third on the program. She watched us do our sound check, and when we were finished she sent a message to us that was a bit of a surprise. She told us we were going to close the show.

Just like at Carnegie Hall, months later, I couldn't believe it. I said to myself, "Is this serious?" The performer who closes a show is highest in the pecking order. It was quite an honor. But, then again, how do you follow her brilliant act?

We returned to the hotel, and everybody got dressed for the performance. On the return to the church hall, the limo had to drive slowly because there were so many people there. There were people standing shoulder-to-shoulder for blocks. There was also a helicopter flying overhead for crowd control.

We finally were able to get into the church, where television crews were chatting with some of the other celebrities. Albertina Walker was among them. I'd worked it out to have Albertina do a set with me. I had arranged to have Stephanie Mills and Tramaine Hawkins, who was a big star in her own right, perform with us. So we rehearsed until it was time for Aretha to go onstage, and I went to watch her. She was great, of course. She was killing the audience.

All of a sudden she calls up Albertina Walker, and Stephanie Mills, and Tramaine. And I'm saying to myself, *Well, maybe she didn't want me here*. I didn't know what to think, because Aretha knew they were going to sing with me and close the show. And by calling these entertainers up early, it kind of destroyed my plans.

Then, just before she finished performing, Aretha says to the audience, "Well, this is my last song. I'm going back and take off these clothes and put on something fresh. Then I'm coming back and I'm going to sit in the audience and listen to Bobby Jones and his New Life." It was just like that.

She said that just as I was thinking that everybody was going to leave when she was done. Who would want to hear me after Aretha left the stage? Those kinds of insecurities have plagued me for most of my life. And although my group didn't say anything, I knew they were feeling the same thing. There was pressure on us.

But then she said what she said, and, of course, no one could leave the auditorium. Aretha changed outfits and, as she had promised, came back and sat in the audience. Not one single person left the hall. It was just amazing to us.

Well, we came out and did our standard opening. Then something special and unexpected happened. One of my girls got into her little preachy mode and the people in the audience got up and started getting with us.

Next, Aretha's son broke out across the front of the hall in a dance. And we looked for Aretha but she wasn't in her seat. There she was, about four rows back. She was also up dancing and waving her hat and clapping her hands.

What a delightful evening this turned out to be for us! We had Aretha and her son dancing in the aisles! Even the reception which followed was magnificent.

Afterward, I went down and talked to Aretha in her office for a while. She told me that she wanted to do more projects with us. She wanted to do AIDS benefits in New York City, Chicago, and Washington, D.C. And, of course, I told her I'd be delighted to do those with her. That's how I ended up at Avery Fisher Hall . . .

24

Pastor T. D. Jakes Offers Me Comfort

Playing Avery Fisher Hall was great, but to see my name on the marquee of the legendary Olympia Theatre in Paris, France, was one of the biggest thrills of my life.

It was 1998 and I had been to Paris before. In 1995 we had done two weeks at the Meridian Hotel. The hotel was located right down the road from the Champs-Élysées and the Arc de Triomphe. I took Vicky Winans with me at that time, and also Merdean Gales and Daryl Coley. That was really an experience.

I remember that opening night three years earlier had been filled with much anticipation. We weren't that well-known in France at the time, so I didn't know how we were going to attract the crowds. But they showed up in big numbers. About three or five hundred people filled the lounge area.

That particular trip set another precedent for me in terms of my performance. I felt I really came into who I am as a singer during those performances in Paris. I still had so many doubts about my ability to deliver that music called gospel. Even after all these years, I was always thinking about my singing ability or lack thereof. The fact that I hadn't done very well selling any of my albums, contributed to those doubts. But that week we packed the house every night and the audiences just loved me. There was even a large contingency from the U.S. Embassy that showed up four out of the five nights.

And their response was just overwhelming. It was very, very good for me and my fellow artists. That trip was a vote of confidence in my singing ability which came at a time when I really needed it in my life. And I really, really appreciated it.

Our performance was so good, the only thing I was disappointed in was that we didn't get a chance to televise it. I was sorry we didn't get the kind of coverage those performances deserved. Anytime you do something that good, you should have press or someone to document it.

So, several years later, in 1998, I returned to Paris by myself. I didn't know how that was going to work out, either, but fortunately it came out right. It was a truly wonderful experience. It was almost an entirely different kind of audience this time because I wasn't the headliner.

But seeing my name on that famous marquee made the trip worthwhile. I felt really good about that. Plus I've always had a special love for Paris. I just love the language. It made being there even more tantalizing. I think I'm going to be speaking French when I get to heaven.

Praying with T. D. Jakes

I'd heard so much about this big black man from South Carolina. People were always asking me, "Did you hear T. D. Jakes preach?" I'm not really a big fan of a whole lot of preachers—especially TV evangelists. There's nothing really stirring about them for me. But his name kept coming up so many times, that I decided to tune into him on the Trinity Broadcasting Network. This was in 1998.

He seemed very good to me, and addressed issues that were relevant to society. I thought that he was highly spiritual. I also noticed that he received an overwhelming response from women—they just flocked to him.

T. D. Jakes interested me, and I thought that I'd like to meet this guy someday. But I didn't know how I would go about doing that, because I didn't go to the kind of activities he promoted.

One day I was on an airplane flying back from some city and there he was, sitting in first class. He was there with his wife, but I really didn't recognize him until the plane got to Nashville. Then I walked over and introduced myself.

"Mr. Jakes, I'm Bobby Jones. It's nice to meet you."

Then he recognized me. We both knew that in our own ways we were making important contributions in the Christian arena. He was very polite and introduced me to his wife. I told him how much I admired his work, and that I would love to do something with him down the line. He said the same thing to me.

It wasn't until a couple of months later that I saw Reverend Jakes again. He had just come out with a new album and his record company wanted to promote it. I was approached by a young lady who was on his staff, and I told her that I'd be glad to help.

When he arrived at the studio, Reverend Jakes and I chatted for a while, and I had the opportunity to learn a few things about him that I hadn't known before. I knew that he was from South Carolina and had started his ministry in a small church. But now I learned that he had moved all of his people down to Dallas where he was now preaching from a large church building. I also learned that we had a mutual friend in common—Theresa Harris, the publisher of *Gospel Today* magazine. One of my backup singers, Beverly Crawford, was also singing with his choir at his revivals and things.

My impression of Reverend Jakes was that he was very much in control. He's very busy and very businesslike. He's a nice guy who projects all the qualities that a minister should project.

Then I went to one of the James Cleveland Gospel Music Workshops of America and T. D. Jakes was speaking there. It was a time when I had just lost my mom. He was onstage telling a certain story about his wife and her mother, and how they had had to embrace his wife's mother when she became sick.

He must have noticed the sad expression on my face. I was thinking about my own mother. And he came over to the table and had prayer with me. That told me a lot about who he was—his kindness. I really appreciated the time he took to do this.

Then we chatted some more about him and his family. He didn't tell me anything earth-shattering. He just talked about his two daughters and his new album—stuff like that. He so much impressed me that I look forward to doing more things with him in the future.

Daryl Coley Wants to Join My Singers

I mentioned that Daryl Coley came with me on one of my trips to Paris, France. This extremely talented artist has performed with me many times. There are voices, and there are exceptional voices, and Daryl has that exceptional voice.

I consider Daryl a personal friend. He's good with me and we get along really well. He's a real trip, but sometimes it's difficult for other people to warm up to him because of his personality. He's kind of intellectual. But that's only his offstage personality.

I know his lovely wife and two children, and he was the first gospel artist to record an album project during one of my gospel Explosions. It was truly exciting for me when Daryl said he wanted to record an album based on his appearances at one of these shows.

Daryl has shared his experiences with me regarding his struggles with "alcohol, drugs, and the flesh." He also opened his heart to me after his manager was murdered. He has a wonderful testimony about how, on both occasions, he found deliverance from the suffering he was experiencing through the Lord.

I remember that he once asked to sing on a regular basis with my unit. We were on the plane flying to Barbados and some other islands at the time. I think he wanted to do it because television has so much to offer gospel-music artists in terms of exposure. And my show's basically the only place where they can be seen around the world.

Daryl Coley is such a phenomenon and such a great guy, that to have him even want to be associated with what I do, was a remarkable honor. He wanted to be one of my New Life Singers! He suggested that to me many times, but I thought he was too great an artist to be singing backup for me. Daryl wasn't the first established star to make such a request. Over the years, I've been asked by many other artists to let them perform with my singers. But there is a time and a place for everything.

I'm Always Striving for Perfection

Despite my disappointments with my albums in the 1990s, to tell you the truth, I was still feeling pretty good about myself. I now knew that television was my niche. I realized that this is what I did best.

I guess I came to understand better who I was. I was a television personality. I viewed my album projects as an extension of my television career, kind of like gravy on the main dish. Look, I'm not going to say that the way my recordings went didn't bother me at all. I like to be successful at everything I do. But I wasn't feeling overwhelmingly devastated the way I once had, over their lack of success.

So, sure, sometimes it bothered me. If there's anything I'm doing that isn't just great, it can make me unhappy. I'm a perfectionist. I want every concert that I give to be perfect. I want everything to be perfect. If the hall isn't full when I go to perform somewhere, and I see these other artists who are filling halls, that little thing would bother me some.

I'm even the same way about the books I write. If the publishing houses hadn't responded positively to my literary efforts, I would have been inwardly devastated. That's because I feel that by now I deserve respect in the marketplace.

I think my latest album, *Just Churchin' It*, is an example of how I'm always striving for perfection. I think it's my best work yet—and it should be! The older you get and the more you do things, the better you should become.

I recorded this album in 1999 on GospoCentric—the same label that my friend Kirk Franklin records on. I saw the success that Vickie Mack Lataillade had with Kirk, so I thought it would be a shoo-in and she would have the ability to make it work for us. You can't say I ever give up trying!

Well, I started out with those high hopes, but we all soon realized that it wasn't going to be the hit that I thought it could be. It was a great record and everybody was on it. But from my perspective, Vickie started to divert her attention to other artists and didn't pay enough attention to this one. And that didn't meet to my satisfaction at all.

The record got up to number seven on the charts, and that felt excellent. I've never been up that far on the charts before. But I had expected it to stay up there and sell more than one hundred thousand units. Unfortunately, that didn't happen.

Vickie has said it may happen the second time around. She said this album was just to set us up to see that we could sell. So I'm working on a new album right now. We'll see. I've been there before.

25

Bringing My Mother to Jesus

I woke up to a sunny spring day that morning of April 7, 1998. How ironic, since this was the day of my mother's funeral and I thought clouds and heavy rain would be more appropriate to the mood I was in. That morning I was feeling as if my life had just come to an end, because my mother was the love of my life. I was hating the thought of having to go through the process of the funeral.

I wasn't staying at our house in Paris, Tennessee, because a lot of my relatives were there and it was too crowded. Instead, I had checked into a hotel where I was now getting dressed for the funeral.

I then proceeded to my house, where I met up with all the members of my family. From there, we headed over to the little Methodist church for the services. Vicky Winans and Albertina Walker walked with me over to that church.

When we arrived, the church was already filled with friends and people who cared about me and my family. I walked over to the open casket and looked at her body. I had dressed her as she always did—immaculately. Her garments were as they should be. They were majestic. Still, in death my mother didn't resemble herself at all.

Standing there and looking at her, I wasn't as overtly emotional as I thought I would be. Halfway through the funeral service the funeral-parlor manager came to me and let me know that there was going to be a delay. The company that makes the protective cover for the casket had neglected to do so. That was a little bit alarming, because all these dignitaries were here waiting to go to the cemetery, and I really didn't want them to see me putting her in the ground without that protective box. So I had to make the announcement that we were going to go ahead and bury her anyway.

It was at the cemetery that I really broke down. It was the realization that a chapter in my life had ended and never would be opened again. Wife, children, nothing could ever take the place of my mother.

For a moment, as I watched her being lowered into the ground, I thought about my brother—and how I had nearly lost him as well. Tears filled my eyes at that memory. That was a horrible experience which took place at just the time my mother was in the hospital in critical condition.

It was at the end of March—a month before my mother died—and there was James lying critically ill in the hospital. I had my niece on one line, crying and telling me about her dad, and my sister on the other line, crying and telling me about my mother.

It was a very, very, serious time and the lowest point ever in my life. I remember how I just cried out to God, "Please, don't take both of them together!" And I know the Lord heard my plea because my brother is still alive and, thank God, is doing relatively well. The Lord was very merciful for letting me have my mother as long as He did, and for sparing my brother's life.

It was amazing when I looked around that cemetery and saw how many gospel-music artists and executives from record companies were there. It was a tremendous show of respect from the gospel-music in-dustry that I will always be grateful for.

They were all there on such short notice. My mother had died on a Saturday, and on Tuesday I had the funeral. That meant that on Sun-day nobody would have been in their offices to find out that my mother had died; they only got the information on Monday. Yet by Monday night they were all there.

Just about every gospel-music record company there was, had sent a representative to the funeral. And so many stars, like Vicky Winans and Albertina Walker, had flown in. Beverly Crawford came and sang at the funeral, and one of my best friends—the Reverend Harold Finch—conducted the service.

In the midst of all my sadness, my heart was lifted by the presence of so many friends. It helped me get through that terrible day. That has been one of the blessings of my life. I am always surrounded by people who love me. And to all these friends, let me say right now that I love you back equally.

Epilogue

I gaze out the window of my home in a suburb of Nashville, and I wonder where the Lord intends me to take this industry and this music in the years to come.

The new millennium has arrived, and I am hopeful that He will continue to allow me to play a vital role in exposing this music to people everywhere. I'm willing and ready to participate and do whatever I can do to make sure that the Good News is spread throughout the world.

I want to let people know that God loves all of us and that all of us are equal in his sight. Our conduit to the perfect order is through Him!

We will reach this perfect order through our own spiritual self-examination. All we need to do is take a good and honest look at our spiritual values—values that include kindness, goodness, love, respect, and decency—and make sure that these values within us are in good shape, spiritually. We need to share all the goodness that God has given us with our brothers and sisters around the world.

In this new millennium, I also hope to continue and expand my Bobby Jones University of Gospel Music. These are retreats I sponsor several times a year for gospel-music artists, record-company executives, and other people involved with gospel music, to explore ways of keeping this industry moving forward on a high level.

And I'm looking forward to continued financial support from the industry for these and other efforts to promote gospel music, including my television show. There were many years during which this kind of financial support and respect was not forthcoming. Those were times when many people did not realize the power of television and what I was trying to accomplish out of my love for gospel music.

But I'm grateful that in the last five years this attitude seems to have changed in the industry. People now recognize that my show is a major marketing tool and a showcase around the world for gospel music, and more time and dollars are now being invested in my program so that my ministry can continue.

I believe that in the near future you will see many more gospel-music programs on television, and this is not a bad development. But I know without any doubt that *Bobby Jones Gospel* is the godfather of gospel-music shows, and that we will be around for many more years, bringing you the best of gospel music.

As I gaze out the window on this beautiful summer day, I reflect upon my past twenty-five years in the gospel-music industry, and can't help but remember all the many relationships I've developed. I think fondly of all the assistance I received from the Black Entertainment Television network, McGraw-Hill publishers, and all the various record companies like Benson, Light, Word, Malaco, and Sparrow. These companies all afforded this unsophisticated kid who grew up in a house on a hill the opportunity to express his creativity in word and song.

Faces of people who have supported me over these years also come to mind—friends like the Minister Louis Farrakhan, the Reverend Jesse Jackson, Barbara Mandrell, Maya Angelou, the Reverend Al Sharpton, and, of course, my very best friends in the gospel-music industry: Albertina Walker, Vickie Winans, and James Moore.

I also think about all my joys and hopes over the years, and the peace and love and goodwill that I've helped spread to many parts of this world through my television ministry. This is what I want to be doing until my final days—bringing the Good News to people everywhere.

I often think about being a black man in this predominantly white country of ours, and that despite all the problems our community still faces here, America has nonetheless been good to me and many other black people.

Like Minister Farrakhan, the Reverend Jackson, and other leaders of the African-American community, I often meditate on what more can be done to help our people. I certainly don't have all the answers, but I do have at least one good suggestion: Take advantage of all the educational opportunities that you can. You can understand why I'm pleased to be a proponent of the importance of getting a good education if you want to advance in life.

One of the best conduits for helping others and ourselves is receiving a good education. I certainly credit my education for helping me achieve all that I have accomplished over the years. I'm the only person in the gospel-music industry, to have two Ph.D.s, and I was the first black television personality to host a nationally syndicated and network gospel show. I am certainly the only African-American to host a television program that is seen worldwide.

This certainly could not have been achieved without God's help and without the assistance of my many mentors throughout the years. They taught me that a trained and disciplined mind enables one to go about setting goals and accomplishing those goals.

Reflecting upon the past twenty-five years in the gospel-music business, I also think about the faces of my audiences and fans who have always been there to support me. Without these millions of loyal fans, there would be no me, because you can't make it by yourself—you have to have someone support what you do. I recognize and appreciate and thank all my fans and supporters who have helped me carry my message throughout the world. God bless you!

As we enter this new millennium, one person I can never forget and often still think about is the true love of my life—and that's my mother! She'll be accompanying me in spirit through the years to come. I know that her spirit will always be there to help and assist me, and to give me guidance and love. I will always love and cherish the memories I had with her. The source of my connection to God is through my mother.

Finally, whoever you are and wherever you may be reading this book, I fervently wish that it helps to direct you on a positive path to your life's goals. I especially want my people—black people—to use this book's message as one more way to strive to become the very best that they can be. I mean this from the very depths of my heart. And I know it can be done through concentrated energy and effort toward everything that is positive.

So let us put aside the drugs and alcohol and violence toward each other that divides and destroys our communities. Let us, instead, follow the good way, the kind way. That is how we can rise to another plateau of pride and self-respect, which is where the Lord has intended us to be.